The North-East Diaries Vol 2

The North-East Diaries Vol 2

Batesy's Tale

J.R. Bates

Names may have been changed to conceal the identity
of certain characters in the book.

http://www.jrbates-author.co.uk

Dedications

___

A big shout-out to the following folk who have given support and encouragement during the writing of this second volume of the 'North-East Diaries' trilogy.

Alan Dickson whose cover artwork sets the tone for the whole book. Many thanks Alan and I hope to use your artwork for the final volume (and the dog book cos you're soooo' good).

Lorraine Bates (her indoors) for support, encouragement and putting up with me on my grumpy days.

Brian Long for support and promotion work.

June Nelson & Catherine Todd for reading and vetting individual chapters and for the regular messages of motivation.

Roly Forman & Alan (Titch) Irving who both feature heavily in a few chapters. I'm sure Titch will be looking down and smiling.

Isobel Wareham and Brenda Nicholson (my Axwell Drive next-door neighbours in the 1950s & 60s)

And finally all the other Blyth folk and BGS folk who have been the motivation behind the North-East Diaries. Thank you all (and mine's a pint).

Just to clarify folks. This volume and the events are how I remember them. If anyone has been included in a situation which is different to their remembrance of the same event then I apologise in advance. One event in particular stands out as one in which I may have used artistic licence and exaggerated the happening. My apologies Mr Page... the cigarettes were returned but not twenty (20) as stated.

And Finally a long overdue mention for my cousins from Dunston Place – Irene (Smallman) and the Meins family – Sylvia, John, Carol, Michael, Ann, Sheila and Joan.

Contents

Author's Introduction

All of the events in this book are true yet none of them are. Ehhh? that's a confusing statement you may think... so allow me to explain.

Every event in this book is true from the perspective of the narrator (author) of this volume. Every event hangs on incidents which actually happened in the journey through life of the narrator and remembered as truthfully as can be recalled. But all incidents may have been viewed differently by other observers of the same event.

For example - two individuals stand at opposite sides of a hill. The first one sees a rocky incline with a steep and dangerous face. The other observer sees a gentle slope with an inviting path winding its way to the summit. Same hill but two conflicting viewpoints and both are true to the individuals. Therefore one should not read this book as a historical offering but more as a life journey seen through the eyes of one person.

Chapter 8 with our two pals running away to London is a case in point. Batesy remembers this so much differently to Roly. We've spoken about it and Roly's version of events dovetail with Batesy's in some of the happenings but are totally different in others. Who's version should be believed? Both of course.

Several names have been changed to protect the identities of certain characters and that in itself signals the limits of autobiography in the writing. That is especially true when writing about friends and family members.

Readers familiar with Blyth will recognise many of the features and locations in the town and many of the locals too. Readers familiar with Newcastle, Hull and Middlesborough will also recognise their fair share.

One of the major difficulties in writing this volume was how to find an appropriate voice for the central character. I hoped to show the reader that the events and happenings are told by a person whose life and experience have taken him away from the streets of Blyth and the north-east. But I also needed to reflect the thoughts and speech patterns of those days and have endeavoured to match the language to the moment in time.

The three old marras in New Deleval were all real people (in case of doubt) and although they are now long gone they are remembered with affection. Tug and his life are visited in a number of chapters but his two pals Mordy and Taps Bob are peripheral figures. Mordy's surname I believe was Mordue and Taps Bob I believe had Tweedy as a surname but I can't state that as fact.

Titch Irving of course takes centre-stage in several of the chapters and the incident in Ridley Park was exactly as remembered by the author.

Several things struck me as I was writing and attempting to capture the language of the day. Political correctness was still many years in the future but the casual way that we referred to each other still sits awkwardly when being written as memory. The everyday cruelty that we inflicted on each other wasn't frowned upon but accepted as just the vernacular of the time. I can remember a 'porky' – 'smelly' – 'snotty' – 'four-eyes' and 'robot' in various childhood years. The robot was a lad with leg-irons who'd had polio but he just accepted his nickname and was part of our gang but we all kept away from him when he joined in the football because he could give you a mighty whack. Even teachers and parents weren't immune to the accepted lingo during those years and would casually refer to the backward school and the dummy lad. I can personally remember a lovely guy who used to come to our door selling out of a suitcase for Blundell's and I'd answer the door and then casually go and tell my mam that the 'darkie with the suitcase' was at the door.

All of the above would be frowned upon today so if in the course of the book I have used any language that would rightly be considered unhealthy in today's climate it is because I wish to be authentic... not shocking.

CHAPTER 1

Until the Twelfth of Never

August 4th - 2011 and it's my 60th birthday. We're sitting in a pub, the Railway Hotel in the town of Tain, Easter Ross, faraway up in the north of Scotland. We'd retired and moved up to the Highlands from Newcastle in 2005 away from the hustle and bustle of city life myself, my wife Lorraine and our Westie companions Bramble and Bruce.

The pub was sparsely populated that afternoon and to be honest it wasn't much of a celebration with just the two of us. But tradition being tradition meant that Lorraine had bought the first round of drinks before handing me my main birthday presents... an adjustable walking stick and a bottle of Glenfiddich 15-year-old single malt. Wow how cool now if I'd had a wee bit too much of the scotch I could use the walking stick to stop me from toppling over. I wasn't overcome with excitement as I unwrapped the walking stick as thoughtful as it had been but nevertheless I went through all of the "Eeeh pet that's exactly what I'd been hoping for. What a really useful pressie," with my fingers tightly crossed behind my back.

That was the day I became an inhabitant of old-man territory and it wasn't a good feeling. Yesterday I was fifty-nine

1

and still a sprightly fellow; today I was sixty and officially a senior citizen. I'd gone from middle-aged to elderly person overnight. But those thoughts aside my glass of Tennant's was now standing empty and froth streaked. My chaser glass was in a similar predicament so it was refill time... and my turn to get a round in.

I didn't pay much attention to the bloke sitting alone and nursing a beer glass on the counter in front of him as I walked over to the bar and ordered from the young barman. "Hi kid can I have a whisky and lemonade in a tall glass, a large Glenfiddich and a pint of Tennant's please."

"Better make that two pints cos you owe me one," said a voice at my side.

That was mighty strange. I turned to face the voice. The man looked familiar but I didn't have a name on the tip of my tongue. Perhaps this face had done some work at our cottage, some fencing possibly when we'd bought the extra land... or maybe he was a neighbour living in one of the more remote properties out on the expanse of low alluvial land known to Tain folk as the Fendom. In that moment I was caught short and not putting a name to a face can be very embarrassing.

"Aye... hi there how are you doing?... it's been a wee while," was all I could muster while I moved the furniture around in my head and trawled through the memory banks.

"Forty years isn't a while... it's a lifetime bonny lad," came the reply.

My brain was clanking and whirring away... and it took quite a while before the penny dropped. Then it clicked, that voice could only belong to one person. Surely not, how in heaven's name could it be?... It was my old mucker and comrade in arms Sidney Brown.

"Sid?... it can't be... Hawky?... what on earth are you doing here?" I stuck out my hand and it was grasped and shaken but with a lack of strength. I was gobsmacked the voice was Hawky's and that was for definite but the face speaking the words had changed so much.

The eyes still held the old twinkle but otherwise he looked pale and gaunt and his hair had disappeared.

"Your hair...?"

"Sold it on eBay," he grinned "Saves going to the barbers... I'm auctioning my teeth next." We both laughed... it was just like old times.

"Anyway you're looking a bit sparse up-top yourself. Seems like yours has done a runner too," he joked.

To be fair he wasn't wrong because my hair had been in retreat for a while as well as changing colour from brown to white so I carried on with the banter. "Shhh, don't let my wife hear that Sid she's short sighted and still thinks she's married to one of the Pretty Things." We laughed again but Hawky's laugh was interrupted by a coughing fit. He took a while to sort himself out, wiping at his mouth with a much-used hanky. I turned to the barman and ordered Sid a refill while he composed himself.

"Sorry mate... not at my best just now." He apologised.

We'd always been able to be straight with each other in our younger days so I came straight out with it.

"What's the crack Sid you're not looking too chipper. Tell me to shut up if you want but how long... and what is it?"

He managed a half-smile as he looked me in the eye then took a few moments out before he replied. "The hair went with the chemo and I've six months left if I'm lucky, twelve months if I'm not... lung cancer... bugger. Never had a cigarette in my life apart from that one time in smoker's corner at Grammar school and it bloody well almost choked me. Ohh aye and that time at the factory but surely not enough to give me this bloody lot."

I smiled back. It wasn't great seeing an old friend in such a state. Hawky was the same age as me but looked at least ten years older. "Think you'd better come and meet my wife then... before you croak." Gallows humour, but Hawky was glad of it. The last thing he needed was tea and sympathy. That wasn't why he was here and I needed to find out what had brought him to this Tain pub on this particular day.

All became clear during the following seven days that Hawky spent with us. My old pal had been on a mission to track me down while he was still able. So Hawky, although protesting indignantly took up residence in our spare bedroom at the insistence of my good wife who had taken an instant liking to my old pal. It was a good decision for all three of us... Sid saved on the hotel charges and Lorraine had someone new to boss around which gave me some welcome respite. In all honesty he perked up in no time at all and some of the old Hawky came shining through. For that long and special week we ended up being his surrogate family.

Lorraine immediately went into chief commander mode and became like a mother hen, clucking around and making sure Sid was constantly stuffed with food or making sure he took his medication, grumping and groaning at him whenever she thought he was overdoing things. Initially Sid wasn't too forthcoming, a little vague and evasive, so I was instructed to give our guest some space and some thinking time. There was to be no grilling and pressure questions. Lorraine made me promise that I'd let the situation mature organically and allow Sid to get his head around the real reason for his visit and until he felt comfortable enough to share. It took a few days but eventually Sid relaxed into the situation.

Our Westies, Bramble and Bruce were also extremely happy with their new guest. They immediately knew a dog person when they sniffed one and would make a beeline for Hawky when he finally emerged from his room each morning. He found himself with two dogs to fuss over and they gloried in it, sitting patiently at his feet like bookends until he pulled himself together sufficiently to say the magic word... 'walkies'. Up they'd jump and the tails would start a wagging as they ran to the door then back again if Sid wasn't being quick enough. Then he'd quickly don his coat, hat and borrowed wellies and off the three of them would go, usually close to lunch time over the fields. They'd wander amongst the gorse bushes and bracken on the hunt for a rabbit to chase or a trail to sniff out.

Sid, although now using a walking stick and not particularly mobile would set out with a grim determination, he was going to give his two new-found pals a good time... come what may. He'd load up with a tennis ball in one pocket and a handful of treats in another... our westies were enjoying every minute and Sid was happy too.

On an evening we talked and laughed and chewed over old times. We visited the past and enjoyed it immensely.

Things came out that I'd completely forgotten about and some of those things were so embarrassing when they were pulled out of the mists of time.

It was on the third evening and without pre-warning if memory serves, that Sid came through to the lounge from his bedroom and dropped a package onto my lap. I hadn't a clue what the package contained and we were certainly not expecting any presents for our hospitality so I gave him a furrowed eyebrow look... a soundless question.

Sid knew from our old times together what that look meant and he gave me a weak smile before beginning his explanation... "I've been writing about our lives Jim... the early days. This is the way that I remember it... it's an important chunk of my life that I would like to be remembered. It's why I'm here, well the main reason. It's my story... and I know it's a bit of an imposition but I need your help to finish it because it's a big bit of your story too."

On opening the fat brown envelope I found that on my knee was a manuscript entitled, 'A Funny Thing Happened in Blyth'. It was neat and tidy, corner stapled into chapters and the title of the first chapter jumped out at me 'Red Rocks', an immediate memory blast from my formative years... when we kids would roam that huge and smelly expanse of colliery waste in my old hometown of Blyth.

"Read it over Jim please. Tell me what you think in the morning but no platitudes for old times' sake... just your honest opinion. I don't want my life to be forgotten or to be meaningless. I want people to remember that Sid Brown once existed." That was all he could manage, he had no more to say and I could feel his pain. There was a distinct tear in his eye as he turned away for the bedroom. A man coming to terms with his own demise and contemplating the final curtain. I was struck dumb but Lorraine gave my hand a squeeze as Sid left the room and that gave me some comfort.

I was more than a little concerned as to what was wanted from me but to be honest Sid's manuscript was a hell of a good read and funny with it. We stayed up late that evening and read it through together. Lorraine couldn't stop chuckling especially at the embarrassing bits that I featured in. It seemed that my old comrade Hawky could really spin a yarn.

We told him as much at the breakfast table.

"Sid... honest opinion, about your story... or memoir or whatever you want to call it, it's good... very good. We both enjoyed it so much and we had to re-read some of the bits... especially about Titch's dad and the fishy thing. I'm surprised Lorraine's giggles didn't wake you up when she was reading that chapter. Oh aye... and the Shona episode, I remember the first part of that with the big lass, but only vaguely because I was kicked out of the dance class to go for a caning. It was an enjoyable read from start to finish... but why did you stop writing when you did?"

Sid didn't answer for a while with a mouthful of fried bread and mushrooms to chew his way through. In that moment I realised what he was facing, what he was struggling with. Just for that one brief instant frozen in time he seemed so lost and alone. He took a while to gather his thoughts then he pulled himself together and smiled a big smile at Lorraine then reached over and gave her hand a squeeze as he swallowed down his food.

"Cancer Jim... is the answer in a nutshell, it crept up and ambushed me as Martha would have said many moons ago. I was in shock for a while... a long while. Then I went through all the doctors and specialists, the second opinions and the quacks during the hopeful phase and that in itself was a rollercoaster. In my own mind I had all these different scenarios playing out. Perhaps I'd be able to fight it and beat it or maybe it was a silly mis-diagnosis from an incompetent consultant... and I did try honestly I did... to keep it all together and fight the good fight. I struggled for month after month then... well what can I say? They called me into an office, a consultant in a pin-stripe suit and a matron in a blue uniform. No eye contact from them. They were both looking at the floor when they gave me the death sentence... so cold and matter of fact. No further treatment was available they told me other than pain medication before the last bit... the palliative care. Shit, Christ, bastard thing."

I was surprised at his cursing, but it didn't faze Lorraine. After so many years in the NHS she was used to the reaction. She gave Sid a smile and put an arm around his shoulder.

"Sid it's a bugger...... such a lot to come to terms with but you're facing what we all have to face eventually. The timing isn't great... unfortunately it never is for any of us but you're handling it with amazing fortitude and we're here for you if you need us... okay?" she paused for a few seconds then gave his shoulder a squeeze. "Just remember Sid that the time that you have left is your time, yours and no-one else's. It's okay to feel down in the dumps... but honestly... and tell me to mind my own business if you want... it's much better when you smile and make every day count... get out of bed and live every day... not die every day. Make each one memorable."

"Memorable for who?"

"For us Sid... your friends... and for those two little rascals that you've taken such a shine to."

Sid seemed taken aback with the logic. "Sorry Lorraine I didn't intend to make your life more difficult with a basket case on your doorstep... I just wanted... well hoped actually that if I could track him down then Jim might help and finish off the book for me. I want it out there so that folk will remember me. I don't have anything else in my life... no family and no friends to speak of at least not anyone close... then I remembered my old pal Jim and we had a whale of a time when we were younger... sort of."

I had to smile at that comment, "A load of rubbish Sid... it was more than that wasn't it? You were my best pal for such a long time until life got buggered up... when did we last see each other?"

Sid thought for a moment. "Your twenty-first birthday when you got arrested for nicking the ship's wheel out of the Steamboat pub opposite the cop-shop. They found you sitting on the car park wall with the wheel around your neck."

"Bloody Potter that was... Alan Potter I think, and I can't remember who else. I was drunk as a monkey and I'd probably only had three pints... it wasn't even me. The buggers sat me on the wall with the ship's wheel around my neck and the police turned up. A night in the cells and I hadn't even done anything. The breakfast was disgusting... scrambled egg that looked like the contents of a bairn's nappy... and they eventually let me go without charge because the landlord got the wheel back and didn't want the hassle."

Sid butted in, "That's not right though is it Jim? The day after the factory fire is the last time we saw each other, 1973... I just remembered."

Lorraine laughed but raised her hand at that point, looking puzzled. "So what's the story here with you two? Jim's never explained. Why did two good pals lose touch for so many years?"

The question landed like a bombshell, unwelcomed, I didn't want to answer that one. The memory of the evening of my twenty-first came flooding back and the whole trauma of the factory fire and it was still raw after all those years, having been locked away in a brain file marked 'Confidential, never to be opened.'

Luckily Sid stepped in. "It was all my fault... the falling out. I opened my big mouth about things which were none of my business... about Jim's sister and the adopted bairn and it broke our friendship, put a distance between us that I thought could never be bridged. Then the big C. gave me a wake-up call and led me here for better or worse.'

Lorraine seemed satisfied with that, but I knew the whole truth of it and I moved on quickly. "Why me Sid? What about your sister Linda, or Milly or even Titch. I've never contemplated doing a book so what makes you think I'm the one to finish off your story?"

Sid went eye to eye with me... intense, "Cos there was a whole bunch of things happened between that first year at Grammar school and that night of your twenty-first. There were loads of other things that you did without me an' all... running away to London... being suspended from school... expelled even. Other things I couldn't write because it could only be your decision to have them out there in the public domain. I remember you walking home from Humford Baths in just your swimming trunks and my jacket because someone had nicked your clothes and bus money. Then there's loads of stuff after that. I tried to track you down once before but I heard you were living in Hull and I didn't know where to start so I gave up after a while. I really need you to be my best pal again Jim... and I don't want to burden you with someone else's problems... but I also need to arrange my own funeral and I'm needing your help to do it."

On my part there were a few moments of jaw-dropping when the enormity of that statement kicked in but I realised at that juncture how important this meeting was to Hawky. He was on a mission... an end-of-life mission and I... for reasons known only to Sid had become his chosen one.

I gave the funeral thing a body swerve because it wasn't fully registering in my head... it was too huge so I digressed. "But me Sid finishing off the book... really? I wouldn't know where to start or what to say."

"You start where I left off Jim... and tell things the way they were. Leave out anything too prickly if it's going to be damaging to you and you don't want to have it out there. You could even change it around a bit... but as close to true as possible and keeping it real. Change the names of any of our friends in dodgy situations who you can't get approval from... simple. It's our memories Jim, your life... and mine too and Milly, Charlie, Titch... all of us. And if you can add a few chapters to mine then carry on and start your own story... your own book perhaps? Honestly Jim, it makes you think of forgotten things... those things that made us the people we've become."

"But, come on Sid there must be someone else...surely."

Sid stared into a distance that only he could see and took a moment out to compose his thoughts. "I can't finish it Jim. I've tried but I really can't. With my current situation it would end up being a depressing read... and the chapters I've sketched out already are happy... funny... about the time when we were kids and didn't have a care in the world. Truth is they were written before I knew there was no hope... you know?"

I nodded... understanding where he was coming from.

"And there isn't anyone else," he continued, "to tell the story, our story. At least not the way it actually happened. My sis Linda lives in Australia and has a bunch of kids and grandkids. She lives near a bloody jungle. Somewhere called Braintree... no-no that's in Essex isn't it? I mean Daintree... in Queensland. I went there once and it was like the wild west... but Linda's happy there and that's the main thing. Then there's Titch but he died a number of years ago. I didn't know until recently when I tried to look him up again. His sister Gillian told me he died quite young in his forties."

That bit of information came like a hammer blow. I was stunned. We'd been good pals for most of our growing up years. "Titch? But last time I saw him he was in the army. No-one ever told me... I can't believe... wow... I don't know what to say."

There was a long silence before Sid, head down began again. "And then Milly passed over three years ago and I know I should have told you before now but I didn't know how to get the words out... even when you were asking about her... I just kept dodging and changing the subject. I'm sorry you two... I should have said. Milly and I met up again in our early twenties when we'd tired of all the wild and stupid things... and within a few months we were married and setting up home together. We didn't have children... because we couldn't and it was Milly who urged me to write about our lives just before she moved on. We'd relocated to Kirkcaldy by then with both of us taking early retirement but she didn't have time to enjoy it. By the way she always spoke well of you... even after all the daft kids' stuff that we went through together and to be fair it's a slice of her story too."

With that final comment, Hawky had in his own inimitable way backed me into a corner and he knew it. He'd been so vague initially and then after days of obfuscation he'd dropped the bombshell about Milly dying.

The outcome was inevitable. "Sorry Sid, so sorry about Milly... I wish we'd kept in touch but the best laid plans of mice and men and all that... well, what can I say?... life just has its own ideas and they get in the way sometimes."

"Precisely," said Sid, holding his arms out to the sides, "Then it brings down the curtain and we fade into the fog of time, forgotten. The lives we lived, the joys we experienced... the successes... the setbacks and the bad stuff. It happened to us Jim, all those things and unless we record our lives and put them down for others to read for good or bad then what? We just become another statistic... a government life expectancy number and perhaps we merit a headstone that no-one ever looks at... or we get a mention in an obituary column that no-one ever reads."

"Well said Sid... well said." Lorraine remarked "No life should be forgotten or disregarded. Jim will give it his best shot. Won't you Jim?"

Even with the benefit of hindsight I don't know what I could have done differently. They had me on the spot... the pair of them and I felt as if I didn't have a choice.

I didn't want to do it to be honest. I was living a decent existence in a beautiful part of the country with a great wife and two feisty Westies and my life was comfortable and paid for. But with those two ganging up there was no more to be said apart from yes. Between the two of them they'd stitched me up and had just decided the next twelve months of my life. I didn't know how I was going to follow on from Sid's notes and writings. No idea if I'd ever be able to complete the ten or twelve thousand words he said was needed to finish the book but now I was committed.

As it turned out I did manage to finish the book before Sid journeyed to the other side and I'd get to read it to him in the hospice... the day before he moved on and I lost a most precious pal. I'd even started another book, The North-East Diaries vol 2... Batesy's Tale – to pick up from where Sid had left off and I'd even become enthusiastic about it remembering the good stuff and the bad.

His last words to me were, "Jim, you've made a good job of it, thank you. But you didn't say anything about Martha dying or Charlie going missing." His voice drifted away for a few minutes, then his eyes opened again, something else recalled.

"And what about Jesus... can you remember how confused we were about those things he said?"

I did remember. One of the mysteries of our early lives. A bloke called Jesus from the Bates Pit timberyard had appeared in our lives and told us things it couldn't have been possible to know. "Aye Sid, I do recall that time, how could I forget?"

"Do you think it was really him... you know, the proper Jesus?"

I couldn't lie to him, he would know. "I'm not sure Sid, I honestly don't know, but I hope so."

"Me too Jim... me too. You should have started your bit of the book with that Jesus day. It's the one that has always stumped me. See if you can fit it in somewhere." And with that he closed his eyes and drifted into slumber. I wasn't to hear his voice again.

I had to re-write several chapters to fulfil my promise to Sid and write about the Jesus episode and I don't know why, but it was probably to save Sid's feelings that I never got around to telling him about my meeting up with Charlie quite unexpectedly in Hull of all places... but that meeting was for my own book and I hope Sid would have approved.

And as for writing my own book 'Batesy's Tale', I struggled for a few weeks with all the memories, I just didn't know which way to handle them but fortunately Lorraine realised something wasn't right and saw that I was wrestling with the past and losing.

When Lorraine had something on her mind she would just come right out with it and deal with the fallout later. So, she sat down beside me at the computer one day and said, "Okay Jim, what's the problem?... you've been like a bear with a sore head and that's not a good trait to have... and it's not very nice for me and the dogs to have to live with it."

I sighed and shrugged, "Aahh... it's nothing really, I just...."

Then zero, I was stuck. The pause and the silence seemed to last for ages.

Lorraine was first to break the impasse, 'You just what, Jim?"

"I just... well you know... get swamped with some of the memories that keep popping up. There's loads of stuff I did back in the day that I've never even told you about. Some of it naughty stuff. None of it seemed important until Sid showed up but if I just pick and choose the nice memories or the funny memories then it just becomes a whitewash... it's exactly like the Forest Gump box of chocolates. Sometimes you have to nibble at the coffee cream and the one with nuts in... you can't just throw them out because you don't like the taste."

"Wow husband of mine, that's some analogy you've just come out with." She chuckled and gave my arm a squeeze. "Just write it Jim... and when you've finished I'll read it, warts and all. You can't change the past and the things that have happened, and anyway there's things I've never told you about too... but I can't write like you. I want to know about the things you got up to before I came along... the things you did with Sid... your meeting up with Charlie again and how he managed to turn your life around. I want to hear about your good times even if they weren't with me and the bad times too. You know, Sid said 'they happened to us Jim... the good things and the bad things' and he was right the past can't be changed to suit our current thinking. Write it Jim, write it... it won't impact on us in any way whatsoever."

That speech was my starting pistol and I began to write like I'd never written before... and it was satisfying. Thank you Lorraine for the soothing words and thank you Sid for planting the idea... because it sprouted and grew and so our story continues.

CHAPTER 2

Bits and Pieces

It was supposed to be the final week of our tenure at the Plessey Road Grammar site and we had been expecting to embark on a new adventure next term at our purpose-built Lego building on Tynedale Drive, Cowpen Estate in a state of the art 'new school'. The building had hit some foundation snags however and in its current state looked more like a kids' Meccano set. So with the holdups it was a long way from completion and relocation had been postponed for the foreseeable future. We'd been informed another year was to be enjoyed in our present school building but even so year-three was to see a splitting of classes... and Sid and I were to be separated anyway. When September term 1964 began I was going to be in 3-west, with all the reprobates... Alan Potter, Tom McDougall, Bill Wandless, Denis (Tex) Tait and a new lad, Mick Marcroft... the smokers and the jokers. I didn't care... my dopey head was in the ascendancy by now.

But to be honest I was now starting to notice girls, and there were some bonny ones, Denise Dixon, Janice Morgan, Helen Ferguson, Lesley Bragg and a hundred others. My head was full of all these different emotions that I didn't know how to control. I found it difficult to talk to anyone who was wearing a skirt. I was now in the blushing when chatting to girls phase of my life.

My ex-pal Sid hadn't attempted to talk to me, not even once during our post-runaway episode and that was perhaps just as well because his voice was breaking and I'd probably have laughed if he'd squeaked at me. My own voice had been through the embarrassing squeaky-groan months but I'd come out of the other end unscathed, and now when I spoke it sounded as if someone else was doing the talking, an older lad. It was weird.

We had still been in the same class since our botched attempt at running away but we were estranged and everyone else in the class knew the circumstances of the situation. Sidney was now knocking around with a different set of lads to my own group.

We studiously avoided each other but in fairness to myself I didn't in any way try to undermine Sid and his direction of travel. I remembered Charlie's words to Sid about revenge being stupid and tried to put the runaway episode to the back of my mind.

Then we came face to face by accident on one of the last days of summer term in the Plessey Road Grammar School porch.

It was lunch time and it was raining heavily outside. I found myself eating my packed lunch on the same long bench in the porch as Sidney. Him at one end and me at the other with just a line of Burberry raincoats hanging between us. There was no-way I was going to instigate a conversation with him but to get up and leave would have made me look childish and in a few weeks' time I would be a teenager... with childish things put behind me. It was quite embarrassing... so we munched on in isolation... both keeping our eyes down and paying diligent attention to our lunch boxes.

For whatever bizarre reason I fixed my eyes on a single green football sock... sitting all lonesome abandoned and dirty in the aisle and my head was telling me that someone from Percy house would be facing a telling off from his mother tonight for losing it. I was wrestling with the decision... do I pick the sock up? Or do I leave it for someone else to pick up?... What if the kid who lost it had 'athletes foot'... would I get 'athletes finger' if I handled it?... My head was busy sorting out the intricacies of the moment and it came as a shock when Sid spoke quite out of the blue. First he cleared his throat noisily and that grabbed my attention, the sock forgotten... then he began.

"That Jesus thing... the one about the insects when we were at Charlie's house... he must've meant the Beatles." His voice wasn't squeaky now. It was the normal Sid voice but a little deeper. I didn't reply.

"So he did three out of three... all of the things he said would happen they did they all happened.'

I kept my silence and with the sock now relegated to trivia I returned my attention to my sandwich and munched on.

He changed the subject. "I'm sorry about what happened Jim... about the stupid running away thing."

I swallowed down my cheese and chutney, taking time before replying... "Forget it Sid it happened, it's past... gone now. Can't change it. It worked out okay in the end... sort of." I was going to leave it at that but Sid had made the effort to speak to me and I didn't want to appear negative. We'd had some good times together and it seemed churlish to forget those times and concentrate on the one bad event.

Before I could speak Sid followed it up, "Me dad died you know... after the accident."

I didn't know what to say. Sid hadn't been close to his dad... but it was still his dad and now my guilt was kicking in. I already knew that his dad had died. Titch had told me and I'd suffered some awful cowardly weeks afterwards... knowing I should have reached out... but hadn't.

"Sorry about that Sid, I should have been more grown up when I first heard but I was still really mad at you... sorry... for not saying anything like."

Sid parroted my earlier words, "Forget it Jim it happened, it's past... gone now. Can't change it." He hadn't added the 'It worked out okay in the end' bit because it obviously hadn't for his dad. We both gave each other a weak smile in acknowledgement. Then there was a brief silence that I felt I needed to fill... with anything... anything at all just to change the conversation and to show how grown-up I'd become during the hiatus.

"What did yer think of Delamotte and the sex talk thingy... that was a bit of a car-crash wasn't it?" I was referring to the much-vaunted sex education lesson which we'd all been looking forward to and giggling about for weeks. It ended up being a damp squib. Our teacher Mr Delamotte in his own inimitable fashion had bottled it, too embarrassed to talk about sex to a class full of giggling youngsters. He ended up talking about plants and their reproductive cycle instead. All of us pre-pubescent lads had been waiting for the real deal information about lasses and their bits and bobs. To be fair the lasses were just as disappointed as us... and were probably much more grown up than the lads about the whole sex thing and had been eager for some proper guidance and grown-up advice... but Delamotte ducked the issue.

"Aye... what was that all about? stamens and pistils, anthers and pollen and stigmas or somethin'... what's that got to do with lads and lasses and havin' bairns an' that?"

I smiled and shrugged, "Dunno' - it might come in handy though Sid... if I'm ever sitting in the back row of the pictures snogging a daffodil."

We both laughed out loud... together just like old times.

"Hello Cassandra... I really like you... I'll show you my pistil if you give me a look at your stamen."

Big guffaws and giggles that went on for ages before Sid held up a hand and became more serious. "I've never done it Jim... you know with a lass. Have you done it?"

The silence that followed was long and more than a tad flustering. That was a truly stupid question. My voice had only just broken and I was still two weeks short of my thirteenth birthday. My closest encounter with sex had been reading through a 'Spick and Span' magazine with topless ladies in it and asking a sailor on leave to get myself and Roly into the Central cinema to see 'The Nudist Story'... which he did reluctantly and we were chucked out after twenty minutes for giggling.

It was Sid who broke the silence and I was thankful. "You haven't done it either Jim... have you?"

The question came as a relief. "I'm not thirteen for another fortnight man Sid of course I haven't done it. Nobody in our year has done it... and anyone who says they have is just makin' stuff up."

"Phew... thought I was the only one," laughed Sid, "Cos some of the lads have been tellin' about their conquests... you know?"

"Sid man don't listen to the idiots who boast about it. Everyone does it... tells made up stuff cos they don't want to be the one left behind. I'm not even thinkin of doin' it afore I'm sixteen cos it's against the law and remember I have a sister who was up the duff at sixteen and now she's got two bairns and no husband. But don't tell anybody what I've just said."

"I won't." then he paused. "Did yer hear about Barney comin' back from the chip shop and that bloke flashing his willy?"

I chuckled, "Aye, Barney hoyed his chips at him and ran away."

"We should go and look for the bloke and if we find him we should duff him up... well if he's not too big... or go to the police if he is."

I shook my head, "We've already been lookin' for him Sid. Two nights running... me and Barney, Alan Potter, Tom MacDougall, Ken Robinson and Bob Harrison. It was daft man all of us running around saying to each other... 'over there, there's a bloke walkin past the chip shop... he looks suspicious let's follow him'. It was a waste of time. He wasn't going to be walking around and flashing his bits with a bunch of kids roamin' the streets was he?"

"Yeh, but Jim man, what if there was just two of us and we kept well away from each other but still in sight... that might do the trick."

"Not a chance Sid, I'm not doing any more nights roamin' the streets lookin' for some bloke and we don't even know what he looks like. Anyway what would happen if he's a proper radgie and he jumps out of some bushes or somethin' then catches me and starts smacking me with his todger. You might be too far away to help. What if he catches you instead and he does some nasty things? I'd be in the bad books again with your mam and I'd get all the blame as per usual."

Sid grinned at the todger reference. "Me mam's gone and got herself a boyfriend." The conversation had changed in an instant. Sid had a brilliant knack for doing that.

"How old is he?"

"Probably forty or somethin' and he's a copper."

"He's not a boy then is he? Anyway, what's your mam doin' with a copper... it's not Marnock is it?"

"Don't be daft this one's a detective from Newcastle, and he's done proper investigating on murders and stuff."

"He must be really clever then."

Sid shook his head, "Aye, everybody thinks that when you say detective, but he's not though... he's as thick as a brick. I can see me mam lookin down at the floor sometimes when he comes out with stupid things. If policemen were more intelligent they'd be binmen. But she still likes him even though he's a bit of a dummy and I don't think he's got a clue how clever mam is."

"Is he okay with you but?"

"Aye, but I don't have much to do with him. I think mam's trying to keep it low key with what happened with dad and that... and our Kenny doesn't even know about him yet so we'll see how that works out."

I'd been thinking over what Sid had just said and it didn't sit right. "Sid, I'm sure you have to be clever to be a detective. I quite fancy it for myself when I leave school."

Sid shook his head, "No Jim, that's not right. When you get to be a polis you just have to learn lots of rules and regulations and say the right words when you're arrestin' someone. And you have to be good at sayin 'what's goin on here then'. Honestly... nae kiddin,' we were in the sittin' room and he was talkin' with mam about a big gang fight in Newcastle that he had to go and sort out and one of the gang blokes had a knife. He said that him and his constable mate tackled the bloke even though they were both putrified. Me mam could hardly keep her laugh in... me neither."

"Putrified?"

"Aye... you know, like something that's rotting but he should have said petrified... cos he meant he was really scared an' that."

"Aahh know that Sid... you didn't need to explain." The putrified reference had whizzed straight over my head. I needed a quick get out.

"Have you been in touch with Charlie?" I did the Sid manoeuvre with a quick change of subject.

"Not for a while... have you?"

"Nah, I've not seen or heard from him since the runnin' away disaster."

Sid put his lunchbox down on the bench and stared hard at the floor. He had something important to say. It took him a little while to get his head around his next words. He looked sad as he spoke.

"Martha died you know just a few months after they moved down south. I got a letter from Charlie and he told me. He said he was empty and lost but he was glad that Martha had moved on to be with their children... and she wasn't in pain anymore."

"Aahh... that's awful Sid. He was like a grandad to you." I purposely didn't say 'like a dad' because of what had happened with Sid's real father.

"He asked after you in his letter... wanting to know if you'd pulled everything together Jim whatever that meant."

"When you write to him Sid tell him that I'm sorry about Martha... and that I hope he's alright."

"I don't know where he is Jim he just vanished."

"Ehhh, vanished... what do you mean?"

"Just vanished... he sold his new house in Sussex shortly after Martha died and now he's living somewhere in Yorkshire but even Helena hasn't got a clue where... or she says she hasn't."

"What's that all about... Charlie wouldn't just vanish?"

"Dunno... I wrote to him to say sorry about Martha but it was Helena who answered the letter. She said he'd gone into meltdown when Martha died and there was no reasoning with him or talkin' to him."

"So, where's Meltdown?"

Sid snorted, "It's not a place man Jim... it's a mental thing. He's lost everything and Helena says he just wants to be left alone and doesn't want to be found. He's looking for some peace in his life."

"That's a bugger."

"Just hope he's happy." said Sid.

"How can he be... when he's just lost his reason for being happy?" I replied instantly with a rare life insight.

Sid shrugged, "He's still got Wilf... our dog and that will be enough... or at least something I hope," he said, "You know what I mean... he's still got another life to care about for now and that will keep him going."

"Aye... suppose so. Still it's a bit sad innit?"

He shrugged again, "Charlie will be alright... I'm sure of it. He'll sit himself down and give himself some of that advice he used to give me." He paused and then did the Sid thing again, changing the subject.

"D'yer fancy coming up to me mam's caravan for a week... up in Coldingham? It's got plenty of room."

"When?" that sounded interesting... I didn't even know that Sid's mam had the kind of money needed to buy a caravan.

"Next week... it'll be mint and just like old times."

I didn't like turning my old pal down but I had to. "Can't do it Sid, I'm going to Crimdon Dene next week with Davey Preston, it's the shipyard trip and his dad works there so I got invited along."

No reply for a few seconds... then, "Aahh okay but we'll probably be goin' up another time as well during the holidays... so maybe another time yehh?" Sid was disappointed because he'd been reaching out to me and it must have seemed like I was slapping his hand away.

"Yehh okay Sid that sounds good but you'll have to let me know the dates cos me dad's booked up for us all to go to Cayton Bay. It's like a cheap holiday they let you have if you work at the pit. Can't remember what week we're going but mam hasn't had a holiday for ages."

Sid looked downcast and I suddenly realised that he'd been missing me as much as I'd been missing him.

"Tell yer what though Sid, I could come around to yours during the holidays and we could go down Blyth to see what comics are in at that shop next to the Travellers."

That cheered him up. "Aye and then on to Seghini's to see if we can bump into Vincent again."

That reply made us both chuckle.

"Vincent's gone. He moved away but I dunno where. Maybe though we could do some bike rides or somethin'... and you can come and see me runnin' in the hundred yards handicap at the Miners' Gala at Croft Park. What do you reckon? we'll have a free box of cakes and stuff."

"Aye, that would be good," Sid smiled, now satisfied that we'd made our peace... then we lapsed into a happy quietness.

The quiet period only lasted for a minute or two before the porch was suddenly busy and noisy again, crammed with the cabbage and mashed potato school dinner crowd now replete with dumplings and bursting with chatter. It wouldn't be long before Sid and I talked again.

CHAPTER 3

Bend Me Shape Me

———————————■———————————

Sid and I managed to cram in a frenetic fortnight together at the tail-end of the 1964 summer holidays. Sid, his mam and sister Linda were living in Salisbury Street by this time... at the top end towards Durban Street but a few doors down and opposite the corner shop.

Most days during that period I would cycle down to Sid's house and park my bike in their back yard beside the toilet and coalhouse. He did come to my house occasionally but mam was usually at home. Sid's mother on the other hand was usually at work and we liked it best when we had the house to ourselves... so Sid's bedroom was our usual hangout.

But on one day in particular I almost decapitated myself on my way to Sid's and all because I was engrossed in my own little dream world. I'd paid a visit to the comic shop beside the Traveller's Rest on Regent St but no decent comics were to be had that day. There wasn't a single Superman or Flash, Aquaman or Justice League to add to my collection. It was disappointing so I set off for Salisbury Street with my head now full of plans for that day's adventures.

I decided on a whim to cycle down the back street then park my bike in its usual place in their backyard and knock at their back door to save time. The trouble being I'd forgotten it was a Monday... washing day, and for some reason I just didn't see the rows of washing lines strung across the lane when I swung into it from Balfour Street and I was pedalling at full pelt. My attention was anywhere other than where it should have been when suddenly... 'wallop'... 'kerraassh'... 'scrunch'. One of the washing lines almost took the top of my head off and I was thrown backwards off my bike, landing in a tangled heap with my bum bone taking the worst of the bashing and the pain was intense. My bike however carried on for a further twenty yards before deciding to lie itself down and wait for me. I was much too grown up for tears now but I certainly felt like crying because I was hurting all over. I lay there prone on the ground for what seemed an age doing my corpse impression... then after a few minutes a grizzled face appeared above me. It was an old woman carrying a washing basket and tutting.

"If yer wanted ter help us hing the weshin' oot hinny yer should hev just asked man." She was smiling and trying to be friendly but I could have gladly given her a good old kick in the bum. I was hurting for heaven's sake and she was making light of it. "Yer not from roond here like... cos yer would hev gone doon the front street... where yer from?"

"Cowpen... Axwell Drive," was all I could muster as I eased myself up.

"Aye... thought yer must hev been from somewhere wi' a back garden. Nee back gardens here bonny lad. Yer need ter be more careful... these weshin' lines are the hard lads of

Blyth," she chuckled to herself as she turned away and began pegging a white shirt to the line. I had no clever replies to come back with as I inched myself to my feet before limping shakily away to pick up my bike which fortunately was still in working order. Fighting back the tears and noticing for the first time the big rip in my jacket I realised that now I'd be in for a proper telling off when mam saw it. I made myself a solemn promise that I'd come back later and chuck some coal at the white shirt... that would teach the clever owld bugger a lesson.

I didn't do the coal chucking thing because I didn't even tell Sid what had just happened. He would have laughed himself silly. But I did squeeze some satisfaction from that day because half an hour later it began to rain heavily and my head filled with visions of a drenched old lady furiously taking wet washing off the clothes line and having to put them through the mangle all over again. God is good sometimes.

So with the rain coming down in sheets we spent that interlude Sid and I singing our heads off to everything that played that day on Radio Caroline, the best ever Pirate of all time. Sid had a new portable radio with a big aerial that pulled out of the top and if you waggled it in the right direction the reception was really good. Portable it was supposed to be but a big awkward piece of kit by today's standards... but we loved it and sang ourselves hoarse.

"Riding along in my automobile... my baby beside me at the wheel".

"Well, baby used to stay out all night long, she made me cry, she done me wrong".

"There is a house in New Orleans, they call the Rising Sun".

"My boy lollipop (doo-doo-doo-doo) you made my heart go giddy-up".

Then Sid picked up his money-box pig, which held a few pennies, to use as maracas when the Stones came on with 'Not Fade Away'... and we sang as if our lives depended on it... and poor Sid couldn't sing for toffee.

"I'm gonna tell you how it's gonna be (chuck y chucky-chuck a chuck-chuck), You're gonna give your love to me" ... Sid on penny pig maracas (chuck y chucky-chuck a chuck-chuck) ... I'm gonna love you night and day (chuck y chucky-chuck a chuck-chuck) ... Well love is love and not fade away." We had the makings of a supergroup that day... Sid on the Jagger maracas and me doing the Brian Jones harmonica riffs on a box of household matches. I often wondered if I'd ever see Sid with his money-box maracas on Juke Box Jury. I didn't of course because Sid never did manage to rid himself of his Evening Chronicle seller voice.

Then the latest release from Manfred Mann, Doo Wah Diddy-Diddy, and we sang until our voices packed in. That was a brilliant day and we sang and listened and laughed until Sid's mam came home from work. That was my cue to shoot off home for my tea and we took leave of each other with arrangements to meet up the following day for the hairpin bend challenge... and I was not looking forward to that.

Sid had dreamed up the idea of the hairpin bend challenge and to be honest I'd tried to think up any old excuse so that I wouldn't have to face it. The hairpin bend was where I'd been involved in a prank a few years previously and

I'd ended up in hospital and then weeks off school. Now Sid had roped in a few of the lads to brave the challenge of doing the descent of the hairpin bend on a bike with no brakes. The hairpin bend was as you'd imagine, a steeply winding, downhill stretch of road between Bebside and Bedlington and the hairpin was precisely that... a hairpin where the road doubled back on itself in the tightest of bends with a canopy of trees on either side of the road. Steep... indeed it was and precarious enough if your bike had decent brakes... but Sid's idea of tackling it with no brakes whatsoever was plain silly and dangerous. What if there was a car or a lorry heading up the hairpin... it would be carnage. I couldn't back out though because it was usually myself who came up with the stupid adventures and perhaps this challenge was coming from the new improved Sidney... suddenly bursting out of his chrysalis like a butterfly, emerging from an awkward childhood.

Unfortunately for myself the weather was good that Tuesday which meant I had to attend the challenge... backing out wasn't an option. So we all met up beside Titch's house on Dene View Drive. Myself and Sid, Titch and a pal called Floppy from PLR, Davey Preston and Mick Pritchard from Bebside and another lad they called Wakey Wakenshaw. Out of the invited twelve there were five no-shows, John Charlton and Geoff Pierce from Grammar school, Scone Laidlaw from PLR and two other lads called Sprotty and Shack who I'd never heard of before.

I didn't question it at the time but Sid turned up on a completely different bike to his usual ride. The one he was riding today was a beaten-up old knacker-job of a cycle that you wouldn't even have let your worst enemy ride. Perhaps Sid's proper bike had a flat tyre or a wonky wheel. I didn't ask but it was a mystery.

So, eventually deciding that no-one else was going to turn up we all set off in a bicycle convoy with our route taking us via Briardale, Patterdale, then Weardale onto Tynedale, past Bebside school and onto Cowpen Road with Kitty Brewster to our right and heading for the railway crossing at Bebside. Then on past the Bebside Inn and Wood's pop plant, then past Harry Harper's place before turning off to go down the Furnace Road and the approach to the hairpin.

I'd been wondering to myself how on earth we were all going to go down the hairpin without brakes... because all our bikes had brakes or so I assumed. So how would anyone be able to prove if any of the others had used their brakes on the way down? It didn't make sense to me... but it was Sid's idea and he must have planned this in advance... surely. Not only that we all had to put a shilling into the pot with the winner of the no-brakes escapade pocketing the lot so we had a gang of very determined cyclists all up for the challenge and all waiting to hear the rules of combat.

And sure enough Sid had planned it in advance. We came to a halt well before the beginning of the downward drop of the hairpin and we pulled into an old abandoned building at the left side of the road. It must have been an old barn or cowshed at some point in the past... and we knew the land it stood on belonged to Harry Harper but nevertheless we congregated outside the building and settled down while Sidney moved to one side to tinker with the cables on his cartoon bike. Problems no doubt.

We'd all brought sandwiches and pop because we'd reckoned on making a day of it but the food and drink didn't make it past the first hour. We sat there just off the road feasting and jabbering away whilst the smokers delved into their secret hidden from mam pockets and brought out their Kensitas and Woodbines and penny books of matches. Titch of course would always try and go one better because he loved the acclaim and he announced that he was onto men's tabs now and he produced a Capstan full strength which he manfully coughed and spluttered his way through. Titch didn't even like smoking that much but we all let him have his moment of glory.

Then came the moment of truth. Sid wheeled his cartoon bike over to the group of lads and I watched with a certain amazement as he took control and laid out the rules of the downhill challenge. This was a completely different Sid to the one who had croaked at last year's running away debacle. For now he was calm, assured and in complete command of the situation. Sid had become a proper Geordie... a proper dyed in the wool Blyth lad and not a single voice was raised in dissent over the rules he laid down that day.

There was to be one bike only Sid informed the gathering and that bike would be the cartoon bike that he'd been disconnecting the brake cables from. He indicated the sad piece of equipment with a grin before launching into the rules of the challenge.

"We'll take it in turns to do a no-brake ride down the hairpin. There's no brakes on the bike and you're not allowed to put your feet down on the ground to slow the bike down. Anything else is allowed... just no brakes and no feet dragging.

The fastest time down to the bridge is the winner and he'll take the dosh. One of you is going to have to sit out the challenge and be the judge and timekeeper at the bottom of the run. Also whoever that is will have to shout out when it's safe to start the next run and making sure there's no cars or lorries or anything coming from the Bedlington side... okay?"

There was no grumbling and no objections to the rules and only one question from Wakey Wakenshaw. "So what happens if the bike gets knacked?"

"Nowt... I can get a croggy back off one of you or a back seater. It doesn't matter if it gets knacked... it's just about knackered already."

"I'll give yer a lift back Sid if the bike's a write-off." I offered.

"Ta Jim aahll hev a back-seater?" Sid was really pushing his luck.

"Nee way Sid... ye can have a croggy or walk yem... it's up ter you. Tha's nee way I'm gannin ter peddle yem standin' up with you sittin' there on the seat and deein' nowt apart from sniffin' me bum." That observation made the lads laugh and even Sid gave it a huge grin.

"Aall right a croggy it is but we'll need to draw straws for who's going to stand down the bottom and be judge. Whoever it is gets his shillin' back and doesn't hev ter dee the challenge. Are we aall agreed?"

Sid had them eating out of the palm of his hand and was in total control. They all agreed and Sid produced a handful of straws from behind his back. "Shortest straw has to be judge and sit this one out... okay?" Everyone nodded acceptance and that was when Sid did me a good turn.

Davey and Titch were the first ones up to pluck one of the straws from Sid's outstretched hand and their selections looked quite long. Then Sid turned to me, his back to the others... and gave me a hard stare as he held out the straws with his free hand covering their length. I went to pluck one out and Sid moved his hand to the left. I tried again and this time he moved his hand the other way. "Howay man Batesy... are yer gan ter pick one or what?" It was the first time he'd called me Batesy for a while and I suddenly realised what he was doing as I went to pick for the third time and his hand didn't move. I pulled out the straw... it was a short one and Sid's hard stare turned into a wink. He knew I didn't want to do the challenge that day and the reason for that... and he was being a spot-on mate. I felt relieved.

The final two pulled out their picks. "Okay lads," Sid announced after checking all the lengths, "It looks like Jim has got the short straw. Sorry about that Jim, nee six bob for you today. Are you okay with being the judge? Cos I know you're disappointed."

"Aye Sid nowt's the bother. Somebody had ter dee it." I conjured up a frustrated face but inside I was chuffed that I had such a good pal. "Let's get on with it," I grumbled as Sid searched in his pocket and came out with my now useless shilling and handed it over with a sly grin accompanying it.

The challenge was all done and dusted within a half-hour. As predicted it was sheer carnage with grazed knees, torn clothes, bashed heads and bloody cuts a-plenty. All the while I stood at the bottom of the incline well out of the way of the stupidity on display that day. It took a few minutes initially before the first of the riders could begin their descent. Three vehicles in a row decided to climb the hairpin... a motorbike, an Austin A40 and a vintage van of indeterminate parentage before I could give the shout for the first rider. Oh my goodness how great it would have been to have had a movie camera.

Wakey Wakenshaw was first and he didn't even make it to the first bend, realising he was going much too fast before jumping off the bike and stumbling along beside it into the trees and bashing his head on a branch.

Pritchard almost made it around the bend before the bike slithered away from underneath him and he hit the ground with a loud thump... his jumper torn as he landed shoulder first, but he leapt to his feet, pretending he hadn't felt a thing... but he had.

I was really fed up by this time, being the judge and the seconds counter. We didn't have a stop watch so when I shouted "GO" at the top of my voice I had to begin counting. "One rhinoceros – two rhinoceros – three rhinoceros... and I was becoming mightily bored with the wildlife.

Floppy came next and he jumped off the bike too but couldn't keep his feet on the downslope and went head over heels into the grass verge. Then it was Davey Preston's turn and he put on a spectacular display. He made it round the first part of the bend but at the speed he was going he couldn't steer the heap of metal around the second part and he shot off the road with the bike ending up in a bush and Davey flying through the air down the bank... looking for all the world like he was auditioning for the parachute regiment. We were all worried that he could be seriously hurt, but after a few seconds he re-appeared, climbing back up the bank with a big smile on his scratched face... his glasses thankfully still intact.

Then the final two, Sid and Titch... and the outcome was a close-run thing. Titch had insisted on going last because he was clever like that watching all the mistakes and the good bits of the other lads.

So Sid it was on the next run and by the rules of the challenge there were no brakes on the bike and putting your feet down wasn't allowed... but you could do anything else that you thought might give you some advantage. Sid although I couldn't see this from the bridge had decided to let the front tyre down almost flat. Then when I gave my starting shout he began to slalom down the bank going from side to side across the road and at some points almost going back on himself, and it worked. It slowed his speed down dramatically and he slalomed his merry way down to my finishing line at the bridge the first rider to do so. By this time I had managed to count a huge herd of rhinoceroses. "Two hundred and three rhinoceros, two hundred and four rhinoceros." Then Sid crossed the line triumphant with his right arm raised in the air in his assumed victory. But Titch was still to go and I had a funny feeling that he wouldn't take defeat without a hell of a fight.

Come the moment of truth and the finale didn't let us down. Floppy had wheeled the bike back up the bank for Titch's final descent and Titch as we were to find out later had also let air out of the rear tyre. Floppy stayed at the top of the bank to keep an eye on the other lads' bikes whilst Titch copied Sid's slalom technique as he made his precarious way down the hairpin. Titch stood up on the pedals all the way down and his legs must have been aching but he was a touch too small for this particular bike and it was too much of a stretch for him to reach the pedals when sitting in the saddle. Down he came slowly, extremely slowly until he'd manoeuvred around the crown of the bend. Time-wise he was way behind Sid's marker but when the straight stretch of the bank appeared in front of him he stopped slaloming and began to pedal like a madman. It was insane he wouldn't be able to stop and the bike was making a screeching noise... running as it was on the wheel rims.

I kept counting as Titch hurtled towards us. "Two hundred rhinoceros" and jumped out of the way as I gave my final "Two hundred and four rhinoceros". Titch screeched past but managed with some gymnastic expertise to fling himself off the bike and land with a thump on the grass verge whilst the bike committed it's final act of the day as it smashed into the bridge wall and the front wheel shot over the side and into the scrub below at the riverbank.

Titch lay there for a while sorting out his breathing and no doubt trying to find out if all the various bits of his body were still in working order.

"Yaa'll right Titch?" I asked as I put out a hand to help him up.

He grasped the hand and pulled himself to his feet. I could see his jeans were all scraped down one side and he had a nasty scratch to his temple. "Aye, aahmm champion man... aahh won didn't aahh?"

"Course yer didn't," it was Sid's voice behind me. "Yer weren't as quick as me man," then he turned to me "That's right isn't it Jim?"

Now I was in a situation I didn't want to be in. To be absolutely honest I just wasn't sure who had the winning time because I'd changed the rhinoceros to horse when I got bored and Sid was coming down then I changed it to mouse when Titch was coming down. So I didn't know who had really won. What to do... problems, problems. One contestant was my recent mate who'd shared some good and bad escapades with me since he'd come on the scene. And Titch, although at a different school now had been a real good pal since Hitler was a lad. I was torn between the two and I wished at that moment that one of them had fallen off half-way up... either one would have done and it would have got me out of this fix.

"Anyway, Titch put his feet on the ground when he was comin' down." From behind me came a comment from Sid that I didn't feel comfortable with. I hadn't seen Titch do any cheating.

But Titch just laughed at the statement "Divvent talk so daft man... my feet don't even reach the ground when I'm standin' up."

That comment from Titch thankfully was the ice-breaker and everyone had a laugh... with Titch, not at him. I declared that as close as I could call it... I thought it was a draw... and I swore that both had crossed the line with exactly the same number of rhinoceroses.

Titch and Sid split the money that day and it was Sid who rode Titch's bike back to Cowpen with Titch on the crossbar.

Although today's event had been stupid in conception a good day was had by all the walking wounded. We would all have a super escapade for the memory banks and many a tall tale would be told when we all returned to school. It did make me wonder if any other idiots ever attempted the hairpin no-brake challenge... and what hospital they attended.

CHAPTER 4

It's Good News Week

The school year of 1964-65 turned out to be a period of incredible highs and depressing lows. Now I was not only a teenager but also a paper-lad for Greener's in Newsham with my round covering New Deleval. My dad had made a point of fixing me up with some work. So now not only did I have more money in my pocket every week but crucially it was also the time when my life began to take on some shape because of my interactions with an old man called 'Tug'. He was a streetwise and utterly confusing old codger who would reshape the way I looked at life. My pal Sid had been transformed by his mentoring from Charlie Chuck and maybe I was searching for someone similar in my life. But I have to say that to a certain extent my times with Tug would mirror Sid's experiences... although not always for the good.

Tug was the old man who marked our papers up prior to delivery, working from an old and empty shop at the top end of Plessey Road. My area covered St Bede's Road, Park Drive, The Oval and all other streets within the limits of Laverock Hall Road and Newcastle Road. It was quite a heavy round but Sundays were particularly heavy and always meant a minimum of two trips to the shop for a refill of the paper-bag. Why folk needed to have two, three or even more newspapers on a Sunday always confused me because by my reckoning they would be reading the same news over and over again. Nevertheless there were many multi-paper Sunday households on my round and some of those newspapers had fat colour supplements.

The old man Tug however seemed to take a liking to me and all because of my dad. I don't think I'd exchanged more than a dozen words with him in those first few weeks while I was trying to fit in but on one evening in particular whilst we were waiting for the overdue Chronicles to be dropped off he said,

"You're Jimmy Bates's laddie aren't you."

"Aye" I replied, wondering how he knew my dad.

"Good bloke your dad... canny foot runner if I remember. He used to do training runs with Albert Spence... and Spence went to the Powderhall".

"Who's Spence?" I asked, "and what's the Powderhall?",

"Spence used to be the best foot-runner in the north-east and it's the pretend name he used to run under. He was in submarines in the war so it's a mystery how he became so fast... but he did and he went on to win the Powderhall sprint. His proper name is Grant, a chiropodist I think... and the Powderhall is in Scotland and it's where you run for money."

That piece of information got me thinking, "So what's the story about that bloke using a false name. Was he a criminal or summat... you know on the run from the coppers?"

"No man of course not it's just the way it was then cos everyone who ran for money used a false name so they could keep their heads down and still run amateur too. Anyway his son goes to your school I think. They call him Carl... but he's maybe younger than you. How come your dad never told you about his running days?"

I just shrugged, "Me dad's always working overtime and that... I don't get to talk to him much and when I do he doesn't say a lot."

"What about your mam then... doesn't she tell you about your dad and his running days?"

"Nah, me mam doesn't talk to me really... she just talks at me. She only speaks to me when she's telling me off or telling me what to do."

Tug grinned, "Aye, well it's the same for most kids," then he paused before coming out with the first of his many nuggets of life insights. "You know Jimmy... life's like a bike... and you have to learn how to ride it... and your mam and dad are your stabilizers. They're just trying to make sure you don't fall off." I was still attempting to digest that statement when the overdue Chronicles arrived and the empty shop was soon full of hustle and bustle and the other eager paper lads. I'd need to give his words some thought.

Meanwhile at school I went through a torrid few weeks. Dropped from Blyth Boys football team as well as the school football team because I'd missed a match against St Wilfred's. I don't even know why I missed the match because I set off on that Saturday morning with my football kit in my haversack... and then somehow in the midst of a head-fuddle I ended up sitting on the beach promenade just staring out at the sea.

Aborigines in Australia would call it 'going walkabout', but I wasn't an Aborigine and the promenade definitely wasn't Australia. We sat there all day my bike and I until it was time to set off for Newsham and do my paper round. My head was in a fog, not for the first time and definitely not the last but having not so much as an inkling that there was something wrong I just blustered through those next few weeks... sometimes angry and provocative... sometimes withdrawn and wretched, I was not in a good place.

It was the Monday following my Saturday walkabout and the same day that Pete Butters my games teacher told me that I wouldn't be playing football for the school or Blyth boys ever again. Apparently missing a match when you'd been selected was a hanging offence and I didn't have a reasonable or believable excuse for my behaviour so punishment must be meted out. Fair enough if ditching me was the sentence I didn't really care, it was their loss and I recall not being particularly bothered... it meant I wouldn't have to clean my football boots so often. Anyhow I decided that when the next games lesson came around if it was football I'd show Butters just what they were missing... unless of course he was barring me from the games lessons too.

That was just the start of that difficult day however because I also had a confrontation with the Grammar school teacher precursors of Starsky and Hutch... Page and Gibson. Why they had me in their sights on that particular day I just didn't know... but they did and it made me angry. I wasn't long past my thirteenth birthday so physically I wouldn't have stood a chance with either of those two even though I thought that Page looked like a meatball with legs. Gibson on the other hand had always been okay with me and I'd never had any serious run-ins with him but today he was acting as Page's wingman. We were all waiting for our last lesson of the day... geography with Mr Wilson... or fat Alec as he was affectionately known and we congregated outside the classroom... waiting to be told to enter.

Then without warning a voice from behind me, "Bates... hands up," I heard as I was pushed up against one of the old heavy-duty radiators in the corridor and when I saw the two teachers hovering there with their motors running... like an idiot I did as I was told and put my hands up in the air. Page began to pat me down just like they do in the police movies when they're searching a suspect for concealed weapons. Page had taught me Latin in my first two years albeit without much success. Whether that was because of my inability to take in information or because Page just wasn't a very good teacher, I don't know. His search of my pockets however was extremely thorough and his grin when he flashed a packet of ten Woodbines in front of my face spoke volumes.

"I'm confiscating these Bates and think yourself lucky that I'm in a good mood and you're not standing in front of the headmaster right now." Gibson hadn't said a word... he just stood behind Page looking threatening like hired muscle in a James Bond movie. At that moment in time if I'd been a couple of years older and my brain had been functioning at its normal capacity I should have told Page to 'soddus-offus' then grabbed the cigarettes back and conjugated various dangly bits of his anatomy. But I didn't and that was it, fait accompli and all over in a matter of moments. The terrible twins turned and walked off triumphant and I was left standing bereft, embarrassed and minus a packet of smokes that I'd worked all week to be able to afford. I'd only bought them that same lunchtime and hadn't even opened them yet because I was late coming back. That wasn't to be the end of it though.

It was my Monday evening paper-round and I'd headed straight from school to Greener's. The papers weren't up and marked yet and it was also magazine day so I had some time to kill. Tug noticed the look on my face... how angry I was feeling.

"Bit of a paddy on yer today Jimmy... hev ye gone and lost a ha'f croon and fund a tanner."

It had taken most of the day for today's events to really sink in but just at that precise moment... even though I was now thirteen and not allowed to cry I found myself once again on the verge of tears. "When aahmm bigger Tug aahmm gannin ter smash that porky pig's face in."

"Keep yer temper man Jimmy... naebody else wants it. Whee's scratched yer face with a raggy fingernail?"

"Ehhh?"

"Whee's vexed ye man?" he had a unique turn of phrase.

Tug calmed me down and I began telling him about my day. I told him everything about the missed football match and the confiscated cigarettes. By the time my paper-bag was filled and I was ready to start delivering Tug had listened and thought it through before unloading his best advice and pointing me in two different directions... leaving the decision about which path to take in my own hands.

Overnight I thought about Tug's advice and his observation that it was very strange that I hadn't been reported to the headmaster. Maybe the two teachers had just run out of smokes and spotted an easy target to replenish their stock. Something about the whole affair was a little smelly he reckoned. I thought so too and by the following day I had decided to ditch the first option. In that scenario I would just abandon the cigarettes, give them up as a bad job and swallow the teacher medicine. I couldn't bring myself to take that path because that would mean those two were going to get away with it and not only that... they would probably come back and do it again.

That route wasn't for me so instead I took the direct option. It was the dodgiest of the two and could easily unravel but I was still extremely annoyed about yesterday... so in my revengeful mind I began to weave a creative fabric and knit it into a splendid garment... or, to put it bluntly... I was about to lie through my teeth. I'd briefed my pal Sid about my intentions and had primed him with some information just in case he was questioned. Then having done all I could to prepare the ground I lurked and waited for my opportunity to confront Mr Page.

Apart from the morning assembly I'd barely had a glimpse of Mr Page all day. So it was early afternoon and the interval between first and second lessons when I finally found the opportunity to put my plan into action. I was ambling along in the upstairs corridor heading for the chemistry lab and who should be coming in the opposite direction but Jacky Page. He was engrossed in some papers in a folder as he walked past and didn't even notice me until I spoke.

"Have the police been to see you yet Mr Page sir?"

Page pulled up sharply then turned and gave me a hard stare. "What did you just say Bates?"

I didn't return the stare, I dropped my eyes, "Just asking if the police have been to see you yet sir... you know about the tabs that you stole yesterday". I began to walk.

"Don't walk away from me boy. What are you talking about?"

"The tabs sir... Woodbines that were my sister's present for my dad's birthday, you stole them."

His reply was instant, "I confiscated them."

"Same thing sir... and you took them in front of my whole class so there's loads of witnesses when the police come."

"Police... police, what on earth are you talking about boy?"

"Me mam said if she couldn't get to the police station today she's going to go tomorrow morning sir when my dad comes in from night shift and she's going to be making a report about the theft."

Mr Page looked stunned and went quiet.

"Me uncle Alfred's a solicitor an' all and he says that in school any bodily searches of children have to be carried out in a private room and witnessed by a responsible adult."

Mr Page was more subdued now. "Mr Gibson witnessed the search."

"I said responsible adult sir," now I was being cocky "And not someone who was going to smoke half of the tabs."

"Birthday present you say?"

"Yes sir... me mam's foamin' and so's me sister... she's really annoyed."

Mr Page looked shocked. I didn't say any more but turned to walk away.

"I'll need to speak to your mother... Bates."

"She'll be here the morra' morning with the coppers sir... you may as well wait until then." Then I did walk away without another word but I could feel his eyes boring into my back.

Greener's shop that same day, late afternoon and Tug was puffing away on one of the cigarettes I'd given him. My ten confiscated tabs had turned into twenty like magic. Mr Page had buttonholed me at the end of my final lesson, pulled me into an empty classroom and handed over two packets of ten Woodbines. Contrition was the order of the day and he said that he'd made a mistake and was sorry because he thought the cigarettes were for me to smoke and hoped that would be the end of the matter... and he said it with a questioning look in his eye.

Pupil bribery and teacher frightery had just reared their ugly heads and my ploy had been successful. I was ecstatic inside... because I was now ten buckshee tabs to the good but I didn't let him off the hook entirely. I said that it wasn't up to me but I reckoned I should be able to talk my mam out of going to the police and I'd tell her that it was an honest mistake. I said I'd let him know the outcome the following day... then moved away quickly because he looked like he was about to kiss me.

"I didn't know you had an uncle who's a solicitor," said Tug whilst blowing out a cloud of smoke.

"Tug I haven't even got an Uncle Alfred never mind him being a solicitor... I lied man."

"Ye were teckin a chance there mind. That could hev dropped ye right in the clarts. Teachers aren't stupid ye knaa,"

"Mine are. Well mevvys not stupid, but Tug you said that bullies always cave in if ye stand up to them. So aah told a few fibs just ter make them scared in case it was true... and ahh scored for ten tabs."

Tug threw me a big grin, "Aye, ahh suppose... but ye better watch yourself noo Jimmy cos they won't forget it," then he paused and thought, "what if they'd gone and asked somebody about yer dad's birthday?"

"Page did... he went to another class that were doing physics and he asked a couple of the lads... but they didn't know what he was talking about. David Harrison told me all about it. Then he asked me pal Sid about me dad's birthday and Sid told him that he didn't know the date but he did know that Batesy's mam was having a surprise party for his dad this Saturday."

"So, is it not your dad's birthday then?"

"Nah, that was two weeks ago... but I'd told Sid what to say."

"Be careful Jimmy... aahmm just sayin'... speshly when ye get other folk involved, because now you owe someone a favour."

"Sid's ok... he wouldn't ever grass. Anyway I told him all about my bad day yesterday. He's had bad days an' all and I've helped him out."

"Fair enough," said Tug philosophically. "Ye have to gan through bad days to appreciate good days... otherwise how do ye knaa?"

I chewed over that last verbal nugget from Tug as I delivered my papers... then having weighed up all the recent happenings I decided that today had definitely been a good day.

CHAPTER 5

We Can Work it Out

———————————————————■———————————————————

Life whizzed by at an alarming rate but somehow I managed to cling on. Unfortunately I was hanging on to an existence that was in a depressing downward spiral. Everything I did seemed to be wrong or to go wrong and all the events outside of my control were going pear shaped too.

Sid informed me that he would be leaving Blyth Grammar School because his mam was to be married again and they would be moving to Morpeth. Sid then proceeded to tell me that he'd already been through his interview for Morpeth Grammar and had been accepted to begin after the Christmas break. He gave me the information one day when we were sitting in his bedroom. I didn't respond. I was disappointed but there was nothing I could say without appearing to be a big jessie. I'd more or less lost regular contact with my other good mate Titch who now had a different set of friends from PLR and now I was to lose my best Grammar pal. To be honest I was gutted but didn't show it.

"Nae bother man Sid, when you get settled I can bike over to Morpeth to see you and you can come over to mine."

Sid raised his eyebrows at that comment because Morpeth wasn't an easy bike ride away and he also knew my house was not a happy place in those days. My sister with two kids and recently divorced was now onto a new bloke from New Deleval and mam and dad were making plans to move out of Axwell into a four-bedroom house when the council offered us one. My sister's new bloke would only be moving in after the move because our Axwell house was overcrowded. Was the new bloke ok? I didn't know but there was information circulating on the local tittle-tattle grapevine. It ended up that he wasn't to be the fella to bring my sister any happiness. We didn't know it at the time but my sister's new romantic interlude would end up in marriage and divorce and in the same dustbin as her first relationship within a few short years.

On that day in particular Sid and I had been making a list of the bonniest lasses at our school. I think we'd been struggling for ideas that day because Sid's radio was on the blink and we couldn't listen to 'Caroline' so Sid had come up with the bonny lass list. I wasn't enthusiastic but it was something to do. Sid and his long-time girlfriend Millie were no longer an item even though they lived next door to each other and Sid had now developed something of a roving eye. It was as if Sid had been released from a straitjacket when Millie finished with him and he was really enthusiastic about playing the field.

We'd both listed our top ten in order in a session that Sid called 'Top of the Paps'... he thought it was funny. The chart hit show - Top of the Pops had its debut in January of that year and had quickly gone on to replace Juke Box Jury and Ready Steady Go as our most popular music programme.

Sid's play on words left me cold but I played along because there was no alternative. Sid had certainly changed in the last year. From having been something of an introverted young lad he'd now emerged as a self-confident teenager but with a streak of unhealthy arrogance.

Then we began, "Who's your number one?" asked Sid, keeping his arm over his own paper.

"Anne Patterson, I think she's deed bonny," I said.

"Fair enough, good pick. I've got her at number eight. My number one is Linda Bamburgh."

"Aye right, but she's goin' out with Potter isn't she?"

"So what? I didn't say they didn't have to have boyfriends."

"Okay then... my number two is Dot Cowan and she's goin out with some lad from Dudley called Mullarky... I think."

"My number two is Ann Savage," said Sid... perusing his list.

"But she's in the year below us. You didn't say we could pick lasses from different years."

"I didn't say that we couldn't either... it doesn't matter. It just has to be lasses that you think are lush." Sid was changing the rules as he went.

"In that case I need to put Linda Winter and Christine Shepherd on my list... oh aye and Ann Savage as well... same as yours."

"Ye can't just pick the same ones as me man Jim cos then we'll not have anything to argue about."

"Okay then I'm pickin' Carol Thomson and Julie Harris, cos they're the two bonniest in Cowpen."

"Naah man... they have ter gan to wor school."

"Who says? You're just mekkin up rules when it suits yer."

"Ner aahmm not."

"Aye ye are."

This interlude wasn't fun by any stretch of the imagination and I was rapidly running out of enthusiasm for my list and picking lasses out. It was boring and Sid's news about Morpeth had put a damper on things for me. To be honest it just felt like we were filling in time with anything at all just to delay the inevitable outcome. Reading out a list of ten lasses had lost its appeal. To be honest I was just completely fed up of putting more into this friendship than I was getting out of it.

"I think I'll shoot off home Sid," I said as I folded up my list and shoved it in my pocket. "I'm not really in the mood for this stuff today."

It was sad really, because as I put on my jacket and prepared to leave I realised that a chasm had opened up between us. We weren't the same people we'd been just a short year ago. We were now on different paths and we both knew it. For the first time in our relationship I felt awkward with my pal and I realised that he felt awkward too. We said our goodbyes that day and it would be some time before we shared any more of those special friendship moments. It would be years in fact.

Then just before Christmas I was suspended from school. I don't know if Tug had been correct about the teachers getting their own back and making me a target but it began to feel like it.

It all kicked off one day in geography lesson when I was battered over the back of the head with an atlas by fat Alec...

and he really swung that volume hard. All because I'd drawn my earth axis at the wrong angle. Fat Alec stood behind me perusing my earth with the wonky axis... then, 'Smmacckk', the atlas hit my head... 'thuummpp', my forehead hit the desk and the classroom went deathly quiet. It hurt physically but my pride was also wounded. There were tears in my eyes and I was enraged.

"Are you stupid or something Bates?" shouted fat Alec with not a hint of an apology in his voice.

I didn't think about what to do next, it just came naturally. I stood up quickly, gathered my books and made for the classroom door. You could have heard a pin drop in the classroom... in fact I don't think any of my classmates were breathing. I was seething.

"Bates, where do you think you're going, sit yourself down." Fat Alec's voice had lowered several decibels and he didn't seem so scary anymore with a hint of uncertainty in his tone. I wasn't in the mood for taking a battering from a teacher after what had happened with Page and Gibson. I think he'd realised that he'd overstepped the mark.

I opened the classroom door and I remembered Tug's advice about bullies. I attempted a smirk at Mr Wilson. "I think I'm going home sir... and as for bein' stupid, it's you that's stupid if you think you're getting away with battering kids." I should have walked at that point but my mouth was full of venom and I sent over the nastiest look I could as I said, "When my dad and the police get here you'll be in for it you fat oink." I stepped out into the corridor and closed the door behind me. There was still not the hint of a squeak from inside the classroom... just a deathly hush and the only sound was the clack of my shoes as I stomped away down the corridor.

Fat Alec caught up with me outside the school gates on Plessey Road and apologised... profusely. Yet another teacher climbdown... and they were becoming a regular unwanted occurrence. He asked me to come back into school but I was still in a strop and I said a few rude and uncalled for things but he was attempting to placate me. Had I been into blackmail I could have made a few bob that day because I believe he was genuinely scared. However, I wasn't and I didn't. I refused to go back into class because I was still annoyed but also because I'd have to face my classmates and at that juncture I honestly think I would have burst into tears. Returning to class would also have looked like a victory for Wilson.

His soothing words didn't wash with me and I told him I was going home and would be back in school tomorrow but I needed to let my mam have a look at my head to see if I needed to go to hospital. I wish I'd had a toilet roll with me that day because when I turned to walk away I saw the expression on Wilson's face and it looked like he had filled his pants.

I was back in school the following day with an Elastoplast on my brow. I didn't need one but I'd put it on myself to cover my pretend war-wound. Mr Wilson made a point of pulling me to one side after assembly and telling me how he had been disappointed when I'd messed up my earth axis because he knew I was so much better than that and was one of his brightest students. I realised his attempt at apology sounded like so much bull... but I believed him because I'd topped the geography classes for my first two years and for some reason I was now underperforming.

I didn't take any further satisfaction from the Wilson confrontation... I just let it drop after telling him I'd decided not to tell my dad. If I had actually told my dad or mam they wouldn't have taken the matter any further anyway and would probably have hit me with an atlas themselves.

Two hours into that day and I was in the headmaster's office. Suspended from school. I'd been caught smoking at first break... not by Page or Gibson but by a prefect. Being caught by a prefect usually meant handing over a tab as a bribe but on this occasion I had been unlucky enough to be caught by a goody-two shoes... and he was just a deputy prefect and he shopped me. Also I was wearing white socks and winklepicker shoes and this too had been duly noted. I only expected a telling off... that was the usual way of things but on that particular day I wasn't in a straight-thinking frame of mind and I just couldn't keep my clever mouth shut.

I stood with head bowed in the office as the headmaster, Mr Lloyd said he was very disappointed with my being caught smoking yet again. I obviously hadn't learned my lesson from the last time I was nabbed. Then he asked me why I was wearing white socks when I was fully aware of the school dress code. I lied and said someone had stolen my mam's washing off the line and I only had one other pair of grey socks and they were in the wash. The Taff wasn't even slightly convinced, he'd spent a lifetime listening to 'dog ate homework' excuses and he'd been lied to far too many times by myself and my cronies to believe my current rubbish.

Then he very pointedly remarked about my winklepicker footwear.

"You know Bates, shoes like those that you're wearing really aren't acceptable for a Grammar school."

That comment really annoyed me because I was wearing the shoes for the first time. I didn't even like them because wedgies were the current foot fashion but mam had bought a pair of winkles from Beanie Watson our neighbour from across the street because her son Don didn't like them. Donny was a year older than me and the shoes were a size too big but they still looked better than my smart but sensible school shoes. So it wasn't my fault at all. It was mam and Beanie Watson to blame for my current plight.

The Taff continued, "Don't you think sensible shoes like these are more in keeping with our school ethos?" He pointed to his own shoes and looked me directly in the eye.

I didn't dare laugh but my brain hadn't managed to filter all the information. I was still annoyed at even being in the headmaster's office and I couldn't stop the words as they hurtled out of my mouth. "Your shoes are very nice sir. Very smart, and I'm sure when I grow up to be an old fart then I'll wear something very similar." I regretted the words immediately.

So, now that canings were on the wane I was instead suspended for the remainder of term for the capital offences of smoking, leaving school without permission, missing a football match, wearing white socks and winklepickers and all finished off with a huge dollop of unnecessary cheek.

I honestly couldn't have cared less at that point. The suspension was meaningless. It was two days before the

Christmas holidays and all I'd miss would be the class party. We weren't doing much in the way of school work and when I came back in January the whole episode would have been forgotten anyway. It did however give me two free days but I didn't dare tell my mam that I was suspended. I kept my fingers crossed hoping that the headmaster wouldn't send a letter to my mam informing her of the suspension. So I spent those two days at Tug's house after pretending to set off for school each morning as per usual. Mam even gave me a half-crown on the second day because I said we didn't need to wear uniform because our class were going to a Christmas concert. She believed me and I felt guilty even as I was buying my smokes at Charlie's shop on Briardale.

It was far too cold to be hanging around the beach and Tug had said I could call in to his place anytime I wanted. So it was off to Tug's house in St Bede's Road and surprisingly I was to find out over those few days that he was a pretty good cook, kept his house clean, loved gardening, kept hens and had a dog of indeterminate breed called Winston. Tug lived alone. He told me his wife had died a few years ago and he just did his stint at the paper shop to fill in time... he wasn't paid much for putting up the papers and he just did it for the company and the conversation.

The bad bit about Tug though was that he made stuff up. He had a unique knack of opening his mouth before he'd engaged his brain. If he didn't know the answer to a question he would make one up like a seventy-year-old Titch. Also he never seemed to have cigarettes... he was constantly on the bum and during those two days it was me who was keeping him sparked up... and I was a school laddie for heaven's sake.

I did ask him why he never had tabs and kept bumming mine and he told me it was the only way he could think of to stop me smoking. I liked him though. He was unique.

How I came to realise that Tug sometimes talked out of his backside was one day when we were talking about school. I'd gone through the whole gamut of emotions, telling him that some of the time I liked school but mainly I hated it and couldn't wait to leave. Tug had responded by telling me that he'd felt the same and had run away to sea at the age of fourteen and it had been the making of him. Then there was a lull in the conversation. We were outside in his back garden where we were feeding the hens.

"D'ye know what a hypotenuse is Tug. It's what we've been learning about at school?"

There was no hesitation from Tug, "Seen loads of them Jimmy when I was working on a paddle-steamer on the Mississippi. Dangerous buggers mind."

"Ehhh?"

"Aye... had to steer the boat around them when we saw one cos they're big buggers and won't shift their backsides even for a ship," then he paused for a think, "I'm tellin' a lie... it was in Africa on the Zambezi where I saw them aye Africa... that's where they live."

"No Tug aah meant like we're learnin' about them and other things called polygons..." but he didn't let me finish.

"Aah knaa all aboot them an' all man. Ye cannit tell me nowt aboot them. Used to breed them right where we're standin' noo Jimmy... kept them in here where the hens are... mind you I had a top on then made of tight mesh ter stop them flyin' off. Made a few bob sellin' them fellas. They used to be popular but they tek some lookin' after so folk soon got fed up with them. Aah believe they've still got one at the Brierdene pub though and it's a good talker... mind you it swears a lot."

I didn't know how to respond to those statements so I kept my own counsel. There was no way I was going to play the clever Grammar school lad and correct Tug about a polygon and hypotenuse so I let it slide.

"Hev ye got yersell a girlfriend yet Jimmy?"

That question came out of the blue but at least it steered the conversation away from mathematics and wildlife.

"Nah... not bothered just now. I used to have one... Marjorie Luke well sort of when I was in first form. Not like a real proper girlfriend cos we just used to pass notes to each other in lessons. Anyway I'm not interested now cos I don't think lasses are worth the trouble man Tug. Me sister's had nowt but bother with blokes and me mam and dad have been arguin' and now me mam's stopped talkin' to me dad."

Tug stopped what he was doing at the hen house and stared away over the back field deep in thought. He seemed to be having a good old think and moving stuff around in his head... then he said.

"Aye lad, nowt worse than a quiet woman... it's just not natural Jimmy. Tell yer dad to mek sure the lids on all the jars in the pantry are on really tight... then yer mam'll hev to start talkin' to him."

Conversation over, advice given even though I hadn't the foggiest what he'd meant about the jars. But now it was paper time and then back home to look forward to Christmas. I decided that I'd buy Tug some tabs for a Christmas box and that thought made me feel better about myself.

CHAPTER 6

(I Can't Get No) Satisfaction

———————————————— ■ ————————————————

Tug received his tabs as a Christmas box and apart from some sort of a present from Greener's I think it was the only gift he got. When I say tabs as a gift what I actually meant was a half-ounce packet of baccy and two packets of tab papers. For heaven's sake I was just a skint paper laddie even though I'd been surprised by the number of Christmas tips I'd received from the customers. Tug seemed to be quite touched when I handed him his present on Christmas Eve... the last day of paper deliveries before a three-day shutdown for us paper lads with Christmas being over a week-end. To be quite honest he looked embarrassed and somewhat taken aback. Tug seemed surprised that one of the paper-lads had thought of him over the festive season. He waited until the other lads had left before he asked me to pop around to see him on Boxing Day if I could spare the time and then he busied away... self-conscious head down and avoiding my glance as he marked up the papers and the last batch of straggler Radio Times and Viewer television magazines.

Now that I was a teenager Christmas Day had lost its magic. Surprises were few and far between and I lay in bed late that day. I discovered in that precise moment that growing up wasn't all that it was cracked up to be. I realised for the first time in my life that I was now looking forward to Christmas dinner more than the opening of gifts. On that particular Christmas there were to be no excited parents watching me tear open presents now so the unwrapping was done all on my lonesome.

There were three LPs that I was happy about and had been hoping for. They were stuck straight onto the Dansette record player in order of preference – The Times They Are a Changin' – Kinks – and Animals. All good so far. There were also the usual presents of books with collected classics in a pretend bookcase to house the ten volumes. Treasure Island, Moby Dick, Robinson Crusoe et al. Some selection boxes, a tab collar shirt and yet another bottle of aftershave made up the tail-end of the pressies. I don't know who the aftershave was from because I never read the gift tags but guessed that it was probably from Aunt Belle. I knew that the 'Guinness Encyclopaedia of Sport' was from my Aunt Mary. Even though she was always short of money she made sure she gave good presents at Christmas.

My one disappointment that Christmas Day was the absence of a parka because all good mods had to wear a parka and mine hadn't materialised. I'd need to save up and become a mod under my own steam.

Then in the blink of an eye... that was it... all over. The usual turkey and trimmings for the family dinner and then a huge selection of baking and trifles for teatime. My mother was a super cook and baker. She kept us clean and well-fed and our house was always super tidy but I did regret that

I could never talk to her and make her listen. There never seemed to be a time during my teenage years when we could make that connection. My sibling sister might remember her differently but I always thought of my mam as someone who had ears but didn't know what they were for... and to be honest my mam probably thought the same about myself. Perhaps all teenagers felt the same.

Looking out of the front window I could see excited kids playing outside and showing off their new bikes, dolls, prams, roller skates or cowboy outfits and I watched them with a feeling of sadness. All the Connor clan were out there with the youngest lad Barry parading around with a cowboy hat and wheeling a toy car around on the pavement. Those happy kids outside had been myself just a year or two ago and I missed the moments they were now experiencing. My own life was in a state of limbo... not a child anymore but nowhere near to being an adult and I was feeling lost. This was a time that I could have done with some guidance and direction but I knew I wasn't likely to receive any at home. The only voice that rang loud in my head at that time belonged to old Tug. Everything else just seemed to be crackly white noise and criticism. So it was to him that I turned for comfort as I headed to his house on that Boxing Day afternoon.

There were no greetings when I arrived that afternoon... other than, "What's that bliddy stink?"

Those were the first words uttered by Tug after I'd parked up my bike, knocked and let myself in through his back door.

"If that's yersell Jimmy ye smell like a tart's handbag," shouted the gravelly voice from the living room.

I walked through from the kitchen... grinning as I found him sitting in his favourite armchair beside the grandfather clock and the black oven range. "It's after shave man Tug... Old Spice."

He gave me a broad grin, obviously pleased that I'd come, "So what've ye got that clarty stuff on for?... aahmm not yer girlfriend man."

I laughed at that comment, "One of me aunties got it for me for Christmas so aah thought aah'd splash some on."

"Yer a Grammar school lad man Jimmy. "The clue's in the label 'after shave'. Ye hev to shave first and then ye put it on. Now ter be fair aah've never looked very close but aahmm sartin there's not a single hair on yer chin."

I didn't know how to respond to that observation so I just grinned and felt my face flush up.

"Thowt yer must have got yersell a lass."

"Nah, aahmm still waitin' for the perfect lass and the perfect date."

"Tha's nee such thing Jimmy... nee such thing... unless yer lucky."

I let the observation lie there unanswered and sat myself down on one of Tug's ladder-back chairs then took out my cigarettes... being very grown-up. "D'ye want a tab Tug?"

Tug answered by reaching into his cardigan pocket and took out a packet of Camel cigarettes. "No Jimmy... it's about time you had one of mine," then tossed a tab over to me.

"Heck man Tug... are ye alright? Cos aahh can run roond and fetch the doctor if yer not feelin' very well."

"Yer a cheeky bugger Jimmy... nee wonder your teachers are always givin' ye grief." He laughed and then gave a grunt as he eased himself out of the armchair, "Howay off yer backside it's time ter feed the livestock." With that he stood up, put on a donkey jacket, buttoned it up and headed out into the garden with myself trailing along behind and still trying to light my Camel as I walked. Tug's dog Winston followed us out. I'd yet to hear a single noise from Winston apart from the odd fart and I reckoned he must be the world's quietest dog. He wasn't friendly and he wasn't unfriendly he just seemed to be happy with his own company and following Tug around.

Tug was a guy who was at his happiest in his back garden and he looked after his hens like a mother looking after her babies. He changed their water regularly, fed them with pellets of some description and vegetable scraps of carrot, cabbage, apple and beet and he would give them little treats of rice and pasta. To be honest I didn't even know what pasta was at that time. We'd certainly never had it in our house except in the tins of spaghetti hoops and that wasn't proper pasta... but Tug told me he'd got a taste for it when he was sailing the world and the ship's cooks would serve it up on a regular basis.

Tug also had a fenced in patch of ground that he called his weed garden where he would let the hens roam for an hour every day. He would throw grain into the weed garden, corn and oats... and give the hens an hour's playtime when they could forage for the grain and the odd worm or tasty weed and be happy ladies. He also showed me how to scrunch up egg shell into tiny bits and then give it back to the hens together with grit as part of their diet to help them digest their food. Of course in return Tug expected a regular supply of eggs which were duly supplied by his happy hens and I have to say that I've never tasted such luscious eggs ever again.

The sad part of course is that I was much happier being around at Tug's house than I was at being in my own home. My house didn't feel like home anymore, I felt more like a lodger. Maybe my constant head mush was a reaction to the chaotic home situation that I wasn't able to handle as a teenager or maybe my head mush was the cause of the problems that I was creating for myself. I certainly didn't have the maturity to dissect the problem and deal with it... so it continued unabated for a long while.

Most days of those winter holidays were spent at Tug's and we used to talk about all manner of things. I would throw up a problem and Tug would give me the benefit of his wisdom and solve it. And we would laugh at life's absurdities but I quickly learned which bits to laugh out loud at and which bits to laugh at inwardly when Tug came out with a comment or solution which I knew to be a load of rubbish.

"Tug, one of my friends called Alan Irving likes to go dancin' at the Roxy and lots of the lasses at school like dancin' an' all but aahh think it's only for cissies. When you were a lad did you ever go dancin'?"

Tug took a while to process the question then nodded, "Aye, of course... in fact aahh was pretty good."

I hadn't expected that reply. It was difficult to imagine Tug holding on to a woman and dancing so I asked, "How did ye learn like... ye know, who showed ye how to dance?"

Tug smiled and took his time before replying. "Well... I was lucky cos I had four older brothers and an older sister."

"So did they teach you how to dance?"

A huge chuckle followed, "Nah man, I learned to dance waiting my turn for the toilet in the morning."

Tug used to come out with pearlers like that and made me laugh out loud sometimes but he also came out with profound stuff that made you think.

I was having my dinner at Tug's three days before the start of the new school term and he threw me a questioning look as I finished my food and pushed the plate away.

"Lost your appetite Jimmy? You've left the sausages."

"Sorry Tug, they look nice an' that but you can have them if ye want. Aahmm not supposed to eat fried things man. They're really bad for you Mrs Pringle says."

Tug frowned, "Who's Mrs Pringle when she's at home? And what d'yer mean sausages are bad for you... is she right in the heed?"

"She's my Aunt Belle's friend and she says that you should only eat fruit and vegetables and nuts cos meat makes your body ill and it makes your arteries go all furry inside."

Tug shook his head, "Not another one, for the love of God Jimmy we've got one of those health loonies roond the corner in Deleval Crescent an' all... and it's a load of horse manure. Ye shouldn't smoke, ye shouldn't drink and ye should gan for lang walks every day. Ye shouldn't enjoy yersell and you should only drink watter and fill yersell up wi' cabbage and sprouts to keep yer bowels workin' proper."

"Aye Tug, spot on, that's zactly what Mrs Pringle says. She says she's as fit as owt and it knocks years off her proper age and she's never had a cold or nowt wrong with her since she started doin' her health eatin'. She says it stops all kinds of nasty things and it keeps ye healthy all yer life."

Tug rapped his knuckles on the table, obviously annoyed and he gave me a long hard glare. "Tekkin notice of folk like that'll scramble your brain for ye man Jimmy. Aahh bet she wears a little roond hat with a hatpin stuck in it and puts it on afore she gans ter church ter tell the vicar where he's gannin' wrang. Them kind of folk just want to stop every bugger else from enjoying life. It's cos they've got stinkin' lives themselves so they want you to have the same. Divvent eat sausages... divvent each chips or chocolate... just eat what rabbits eat and ye'll be healthy for ever... divvent drink beer or pop, just watter and milk." Tug paused his rant for a second then grinned, "Anyway Jimmy just think aboot how stupid that woman's gannin to feel when she's lyin' in hospital dyin' of nowt."

That comment made me think. It wouldn't be until much later when I went over it in my head that it made me laugh. I gave Tug a big grin though and pulled the plate back in front of me and attacked the sausages.

I went back to Tug's for my tea as well when I'd finished my papers then gave him a hand to make sure the hens were all comfy and cosy and secure for the night. Tug told me that he'd seen the occasional fox which had sneaked in from the countryside during the night and tried to get into the hen house... but Tug had his hen coop as secure as Fort Knox so that old fox would always leave disappointed.

Then I took my leave and told Tug it would be a while before I could come back so regularly. The new school term was beginning on Monday, my bike needed some serious attention and I was needing to reconnect with some of my school pals. Tug wasn't a relative or anything but I found myself worrying about him living on his own. So before I left I asked...

"What're you gonna be doin' when aahmm not here Tug?"

He shrugged, "Well it's ower cold ter gan and meet up wi me owld pals up the lonnen and there's nowt much ter dee at me allotment so aah'll just bide in the hoose and see if aah can manage ter get any owlder."

"Aahh didn't know ye had an allotment Tug... or ye gan meetin' up with pals. Ye never said nowt about that."

Tug seemed a little miffed at those words. "Yer not me mam ye knaa and aahh dee knaa how ter live on me tod. Aahh divvent have ter tell ye everything man. Anyways aahmm an owld man for heaven's sake Jimmy. So me answer to yer first question. Aahll be deein' nowt."

The news about his allotment and his old chums was something of a surprise so I said, "Aahmm not bein' nosey or owt Tug... aah was just wonderin' what you're gonna be deein' with yoursel."

"Aahh just told ye man, nowt is what aall be deein'."

Tug was a little terse and I wasn't getting much of a response and I really didn't want to be intrusive so I let it drop with a final comment as I buttoned up my jacket, "That's daft that man Tug... ye cannit just sit there deein nowt aall day."

Tug gave a little chuckle. "Ye divvent understand man Jimmy... deein nowt's a canny hard thing ter dee... cos ye nivvor knaa when yer finished."

That final comment had me chuckling all the way through the fields from Newsham to Cowpen as I biked home. My Tug interlude was over for the time being and now it was back to reality... yuk.

CHAPTER 7

Street Fighting Man

―――――――――――――――――――● ―――――――――――――――――――

So into January and that 1965 spring term was to turn out memorable for a number of reasons. Primarily for the seemingly unending series of fights and altercations taking place among school-age lads all over Blyth. Every week there seemed to be news about some argy-bargy or battle-royal taking place at one of the schools or youth clubs around the town. That fact in itself was way out of the ordinary but guess who was involved in a number of those tussles? Yep, sure enough it was our very own Wilf Rees. Wilf was the older lad who'd been invaluable to us first-formers during our first few weeks at BGS with his insights and guidance that was to stand us in good stead... and thanks for that. But not only was he good at all the school stuff but it turned out he was also very handy in a scrap. Was there no end to this lads talents?

Wilf Rees was one of those folk whom it was truly difficult to like. Not that I'd ever had a run-in or altercation with him. He was two or three years above us at school and had a cousin in our year... Tony Morey and that fact in itself should have made him acceptable but as I say... it was so difficult to like the lad because he was exceptionally good at everything.

Football, cricket, athletics, tennis, education... and one of
the leaders in the cadet corps. The list just went on and
on and I'd even expected to see his name as captain of the
school netball team. That didn't happen for some reason. So
my attitude towards Wilf was in all honesty mostly powered
by jealousy and envy... because surely no-one deserved to be
good at every damn thing. But he was.

So, Blyth bus-station... late January and late afternoon
with half a dozen of our age group stood in a kind of
astonishment as across the road on the grassy piece of land at
the side of the Central Methodist Church there was a fight in
progress. The combatants were Bill Taggart, erstwhile leader
of the Cowpen gang troopers in their warfare with the Bella
gang versus his opponent Wilf Rees, Blyth Grammar school
superstar and overachiever. We gawped as they went at it
hammer and tongs and tearing lumps out of each other...
or should I say Wilf was tearing lumps out of Bill Taggart.
That made it a difficult situation for me because I found
myself in something of a cleft stick. I was standing with all
my Grammar School peers and they're cheering for Wilf
Rees. Fair enough, but he's fighting with my neighbour and
leader of the Cowpen gang Bill Taggart. Who should I cheer
for? I was torn. So, standing at the back of the group I just
kept my head down and gave a few half-hearted appreciative
noises which could have been construed as supporting either
of the combatants as long as I kept my neutrality a secret.
That battle came to a swift conclusion but just as soon as
Wilf had seen off one adversary another one appeared from
the gent's toilet block beside the garage. Fight number two
ensued... Wilf now battling Moya Larsson and to be honest

I turned and walked away before the conclusion because it had become so tormenting to be torn between adversaries. It was a bit like watching cavalry and redskin movies because I knew that I should be cheering for Custer but I wanted Sitting Bull and Crazy Horse to be victorious too.

That same week at school... Wilf Rees again in an argy-bargy on the football pitch with a lad twice the size of him and sporting a headful of red hair. Bish-bash-bosh and they were getting stuck into each other and all because Wilf had decided to come to the aid of one of his less physically capable classmates whose football had been requisitioned by the big ginger lad. That made it even worse for me now because Wilf Rees wasn't just sporty, tough and clever... he had also turned into Robin Hood... grrr that lad was annoying.

Other schools were at it too and over at PLR Derek Raisbeck and Scone Laidlaw had been battering each other's nose ends. Similarly at Newlands... Bob Harrison and a lad called Archie had decided to settle their differences with the old fisticuffs. There were fights a-plenty at Bebside school but there it was the same name which kept cropping up... Jim White. Over at St Wilfred's there were blood-curdling tales circulating of the various fights and escapades featuring a lad called Terry Hall and a gang called 'The Multitude'. Add to those the various skirmishes outside the YMCA and the newly opened 'Centre 64' and it seemed as if Blyth was a town of teenage tearaways.

Home life for me at that time and for a variety of reasons was terrible and it continued in the same vein as we wound our way to the Easter holidays. School life too was a pain in the neck even though I was keeping my head down and attempting to keep myself out of trouble. So more and more of my time was spent at Tugs house when the opportunity presented itself. It was a welcome escape from life's vagaries but increasingly it also became a period when Tug became very vocal in his condemnation of my school and the Grammar school system in general. Conversations invariably followed the same pattern.

It was Easter Saturday... and Good Friday had been disappointing. I was too old for Easter eggs now so bars of chocolate and gifts of money had to suffice and even they had been in short supply. But at Tugs house I received an unexpected surprise. Not a big money present... but a little welcome surprise that brought a smile to my face.

"Here Jimmy... thought yer might like these," said Tug after I'd parked up my bike... let myself in through the kitchen door before coming through and sitting myself down at the big old heavy central table in his sitting room. He handed me the bottom half of a cardboard Co-op egg box with three painted paste eggs sitting silently in their respective compartments before he turned away self-consciously.

I could feel Tug's awkwardness but I didn't assuage it when I said, "What's this in aid of Tug man?... aahmm not yer girlfriend."

Tug was glad of the response. The last thing he would have wanted was an over effusive bout of gratefulness and thank-you-kindly rubbish. "Aah've got nee money for them chocolate fellas but aahh thought yer might like eggs that we used ter have as kids."

"Ta Tug," was all I could manage because the painted eggs looked brilliant. Surely he couldn't have done them himself. The egg to the left was a red Indian chief with a feathered headdress made of snipped chicken feathers, the one to the right was like Captain Pugwash with a painted beard and a little cardboard pirate hat and the middle egg was a fantastic representation of an oval Gina Lollobrigida with red painted lips. The eggs were so fantastic. I was about to say something but Tug jumped in first.

"Ye can eat the Indian and the pirate but watch oot for the one in the middle cos she might end up eatin' you." Tug cracked up laughing at his own humour and it lasted for a good few seconds.

"Where did ye get them Tug?" I couldn't believe he'd done them.

"Off me hens... where d'yer think?"

"No man... aahh mean who painted them for ye?"

"Naebody... aahh painted them meself."

"Aye... as if. Ye never told me that you could do paintin' and stuff and them eggs are ower good. Did ye buy them?"

"Aahh told ye Jimmy man, aah've nae spare money for buyin' eggs. Aahh painted them meself and aahh didn't tell ye about me paintin' cos it nivvor came up in conversation."

This old bloke was full of surprises because those painted paste eggs were really impressive. "Have ye done any other paintin' Tug... any other stuff that I could see... ye know, like proper paintin'... portraits of people or arty things like Picasso or that bloke with one lug?"

Tug gave it a moment's thought, "Ye could come doon ter me cousin's hoose in Shelley Crescent the morra if ye like and hev a look."

"Is that where you keep your portraits and stuff?"

"Nah... but ye said you wanted to see me paintin' and aahh just done my cousin's skirting boards last week. Med a right canny job of it an' all."

You couldn't help but laugh at the old bugger and I did have a chuckle at that. Also I had decided to leave the eggs in their box because there was no way that I was going to crack them open and eat them until I'd showed them around to my pals. I thought they were little works of art. So we sat quietly for a few minutes after sparking up a couple of tabs. It was Tug who eventually broke the silence.

"What've ye been deein at school afore the holidays Jimmy?"

"Same old things Tug... I'm playin chess now at dinner times. We've got a chess club and Mr Reekie's been teachin' us Queen's gambit and stuff. Then just the normal things like English, History, Geography, Maths."

Tug gave me a puzzled look "What for?"

"What d'yer mean... what for? To learn stuff obviously."

"Aye Jimmy... but what's them lessons for?"

To my mind Tug wasn't making any sense. I was in Grammar school and learning grammar things. Surely it couldn't be that difficult to comprehend. So I replied, "Aahh don't understand what yer mean Tug... school's for learnin' things and I'm doing algebra in me maths lessons and I'm doin' the Plantagenets in history... ooohh aye and we're learnin' about the Laurentian shield in geography... that's in Canada like."

"Aye Jimmy I hear what you're sayin' but what good is that larnin' goin' to do for ye in real life."

"Ehhh?"

"Are ye goin' ter be a teacher when you leave school?"

I hadn't a clue what Tug was digging away at. Me... a teacher, as if. "No man Tug, me a teacher... not a chance. I'll probably be a policeman or somethin', maybe a postie or even a writer... ye know like a reporter or summat."

Tug took a huge drag on his tab... formed his lips in a circle and began puffing out smoke rings as he thought about my answer. Deep in thought and about ten smoke rings later he began to dismantle all of my preconceived notions about the benefits of Grammar school.

"So what are ye botherin' wi' algebra for? Cos believe me Jimmy there's nee such thing in real life. Unless you know different of course but I have ter say that I've nivvor once used algebra all the time aah've been alive and aah divvent knaa of a single person who's ever used it either."

I wasn't sure how to answer... I was a wee bit defensive so I just said, "Me teachers think it's important stuff Tug."

A little snort from Tug... then, "X plus Y equals Z squared... what's that aall aboot man? Out of five hundred people at your school there'll only be one kid who ever uses algebra in their entire life and that kid will end up usin' it ter be a maths teacher. Then he'll be able to stand up and look clever in front of a class full of kids while he teaches them algebra... and not one of them will ever use it again in their life... never ever. It's pointless man and yer wastin' yer time wi that carry-on."

I didn't know how to respond to that because it made a lot of sense. Tug gave me a few moments but when I didn't reply he dived in again.

"Ye knaa them Plantagenets that yer on aboot?"

"Aye, what about them?"

"D'yer get on with them?"

"What?"

"Ye knaa… are they aall reet."

"Tug man howay, are ye takin' the mick… they're aall deed man. They're the old kings of England. They started with Henry-II hundreds of years ago."

"Aye 1154 if aahmm not mistaken."

That statement came as a surprise and threw me somewhat. "How did ye know that Tug… about Henry the second?"

Tug exhaled his final cloud of smoke as he stubbed out his cigarette and then gave a chuckle, "He was in my class at school."

He was taking the mick, winding me up but I was still a little confused as to how he knew about Henry II. "Very funny Tug, but how do you know about the dates and that."

"Jimmy man d'yer really think that the only folk that knaa things are the ones gannin ter Grammar school? Anyways… it's just somethin' I heard once and remembered. That's the first time in my life that I've ever used that memory. It's another example of useless information unless you're gannin' ter be a history teacher. Are ye gannin' to be a history teacher?"

"Of course not."

"So… you're spendin' hours every week larnin' stuff aboot deed folk and what battles they fought and how many bairns they had. None of it is any use ter ye unless you're gannin to be a history teacher who's gannin to fill more kids heeds wi' useless clarts. Pointless Jimmy… absolutely pointless. Ye should be larnin' things that's gannin ter be useful for ye."

Tug had me on the back foot... "Like what?"

Tug took a few moments out for a think before replying, "D'yer knaa how ter change a plug and what kind of fuse ter use?"

"Nah... not really."

"D'yer knaa how ter pluck a chicken or how ter dee wallpapering?"

"Ermmm... aahmm just a kid man Tug."

"D'yer knaa how ter skin a rabbit or gut a fish or open a bank account or when ter plant taties?"

"Tug man...."

"Nivvor mind Tug man... whee cares if a million years ago some bloke got an arrow in his eye or if a triangle is Isosceles or scalene or if ye knaa aboot the Laurentian shield thoosands of miles away? but ye probably divvent knaa the names of the main streets doon Blyth. Yon Grammar school doesn't teach yer a damn thing aboot life and the skills ye need to survive in this world."

Tug was on a mission and I was conflicted. What he was saying made a lot of sense but I also felt defensive about the very school which was giving me such a load of grief at that time. I didn't know how to respond. What did Tug expect me to do... jack in at school and get a job gutting fish?

"Ye've gone quiet Jimmy." Tug gave me a questioning look as he stuck another tab in his mouth and lit it.

I let him finish before replying. "What school did you go to Tug?"

He gave a shrug, "Not a good 'un... sartinly not a good 'un," he said as he puffed out another smoke ring, "Which school aahh went to doesn't matter... it's not important, but I can remember it like it was yesterday."

"So what was it like?" in the olden days," I asked in an attempt to refocus the conversation.

He smiled, "Olden days is right... aye sartinly right... and not the happiest time of me life ter be honest... aahh was a five-year-old but I can still mind me forst day at school as clear as a bell."

"So... are ye gannin to tell us what it was like?"

Tug took a while to respond. With a faraway look in his eye he seemed to be plodging around in a swamp of memories and he'd become stuck. After a long minute he seemed to come back to reality then took great pleasure in drawing deeply on his cigarette and exhaling a cloud before replying.

"Me mother walked us to school on that first mornin'. I can still feel her hand wrapped roond mine and her clothes smelt of fresh baked bread. She was forever baking ter feed us all and she always smelt like that, stotties and crusty loaves ye knaa...? Anyways true story and nee kiddin'... she walked me ter school that first day and aahh remember sayin' to her... mam how long have aahh ter gan ter school for?"

"Only until you're twelve" she says, "cos in them days ye' left school at twelve. Ye could still gan doon the pit at twelve then. It didn't gan up to fourteen until after the first war. So anyway she gives me a little mam punch on the shoulder cos there was nee kissin' and cuddlin' back in the day. Then aahh walk through the school gates... and me mam turns roond ter walk away and aahmm feelin' frightened so aahh stand there shakin' and aahmm shoutin' after her... mam divvent forget ter come back and fetch us when aahmm twelve."

We ended up laughing together Tug and I and no more was said about Tug's anti-Grammar school tirade. We put it on the back shelf to be revisited at a later date but when I left that day it began a chain of thought which would lead indirectly to my next notable escapade.

CHAPTER 8

We Gotta Get Outa This Place

Running away from home isn't easy. I say that with the voice of experience because my first attempt many months previously had fizzled out within a matter of hours. Actually it had been my pal Sid's attempt and he'd only pulled me into his scheme the evening before it was due to happen so it all fell apart rather quickly. That debacle taught me that a full-on serious bash at running off for a new life takes a major amount of groundwork and so this, my second attempt had been in the planning for several weeks. It had been fomenting in the back of my mind since Tug had told me about his running away to sea days and then going on to belittle the standard of my education at Grammar school. Those things however weren't the catalyst for my decision to abandon Cowpen and head for the glamour of London. No... that deciding moment came one day in July when I heard the first few lines of the latest offering from The Animals, 'We Gotta Get Outa This Place'. Those words struck an immediate chord with me and gave my plans some focus and clarity.

'In this dirty old part of the city

Where the sun refused to shine

People tell me there ain't no use in tryin'

Infiltrating my brain those words sounded as if Eric Burdon was singing about me and my home situation and over the next few days those lines kick-started the detailed planning of my latest stunt.

"Mam is it all right if I go camping with the YMCA."

"When?" was the sum total of her reply as she stood at the kitchen sink, peeling potatoes.

"Second week of the holidays."

"August?"

"Aye."

"How long for?"

"A week."

"Where to?"

"Otterburn."

"What about your birthday?"

"We go away on Friday the 6th two days after me birthday."

She gave it a few moments thought, "Aye okay," and that was the end of the conversation... and probably the longest chat we'd had for months.

That galvanized my planning and I even surprised myself because it was so meticulous. A colleague from school Joe Dawson who lived in Brandon Close and was a year older than myself was eased into my paper round. Even though I was about to run off to London and begin my new life I didn't want to let Greener's down... and especially not Tug.

Leaving two days after my birthday meant that I'd have birthday money from my mam and aunties as well as my final paper-round money. Mam had asked what I wanted for my birthday and I'd told her I would like a Parka but I would like to pick my own. She winced when I told her how much a good one cost but after a while she agreed to give me the cash to do my own Parka shopping. That Parka would never see the light of day but with all the other bits and bobs of cash I now had the stake money for my new life.

I also had a proper rucksack which my sister's new fella had borrowed from his brother Sid. I had a little primus stove, a torch and a 'skin-deep' sleeping bag which was little more than a plastic bag and when rolled up it was about the same size as a Christmas Yule log. Spare socks, t-shirt, y-fronts and jeans... a map and a compass... some bits and pieces of food to see me through the first day or two and 20 Park Drive cigarettes and 3 books of matches tucked away in a side pocket of the rucksack... cos no self-respecting fourteen-year-old would bugger off from home without his tabs.

The plan was uncomplicated... straightforward and simple. Take the number six bus to Newcastle then after alighting at the Haymarket walk down to Central Station and check out the London trains. Sneak on without a ticket and keep myself out of sight of the inspector. Then when I'd made it to Kings Cross I would set about looking for a cheap bed-and-breakfast place or a youth hostel. Failing that I'd look for a local park to spend the night. It was August and the weather was warm and dry so curling up amongst some bushes wouldn't be a problem. Then the following day and pretending to be fifteen I'd go looking for work... a market stall maybe or a chip shop or something. London was big so there must be lots of jobs going and I knew that my cash stash would rapidly deplete and I would need to begin earning money to find a cheap place to live. Staying too long at a youth hostel wouldn't be a good idea because at some stage the police would be looking for me and that would be one of their first ports of call.

My most brilliant piece of subterfuge however was so well thought out that I sometimes think that I must have been imagining it. But not so. In my jacket pocket I had an envelope which I'd written out myself and it was addressed to Peter Butters, 77 Disraeli Street, Blyth, Northumberland. I'd even put a proper stamp in the corner and cancelled it with a bit of a billy-stamper transfer and it looked like a postmark unless inspected really closely. The envelope itself had been scrunched up, folded and the top ripped open to look as if it had actually been posted. All fictitious of course. Peter Butters was my games teacher at school and I didn't have a clue where he actually lived. Inside the envelope was a brief letter handwritten by myself and headed with a London address. The note said something like 'Looking forward to seeing you next week Peter and we hope your mam gets well soon. Love from Aunt Sally and Uncle Bert'. I was well impressed with my handiwork.

A stroke of genius that letter... because if the inspector nabbed me on the train I would tell him that I'd lost my ticket. He would then proceed to take down my details so that the train people could send out a bill for the train fare. When asked for identification I would then produce the bogus envelope and letter which would prove who I was and my home address... I mean... how clever was that? However, someone living at 77 Disraeli Street would be in for an almighty shock and a load of British Rail hassle.

So, come the day of the great escape and there hadn't been a single blip in the planning or execution up to that point. Even as I left the house I didn't make a big thing about the goodbyes... nothing that would have suggested anything other than a fourteen-year-old lad going off for a week's camping with his pals and the YMCA. Had I been daft enough to do a big farewell scene and put my arms around my mam she would have immediately smelled a rat and kicked off... 'What ye playin at...what's gannin' on here? What've yer been up to? Howay ye might as weel tell us noo cos aall find oot anyway.' Expressions of affection weren't standard fare in our house.

I did however manage to say goodbye to my sister's older bairn Billy. I felt so sorry for him because he looked like a little monkey but I looked forward to the day when he would be released into the wild. I thought about slipping him a banana before I walked out of the front door for what I thought would be the final time but decided against it. I patted his head and said, "Goodbye little fella have yourself a good life." Billy grinned and replied "Ooo-Ooo".

Everything was low key even though my stomach was hosting about a million butterflies and I purposefully didn't even glance back as I shut the front garden gate as I left and headed off up Axwell Drive.

The final clincher for my running off had been the unwelcome news that we were to be moving house during those summer holidays into 14 Hortondale Grove, a four bedroomed house with a bay window. This new house was just around the corner in the next street. This of course was in addition to the fact that we'd said goodbye to Plessey Road and the following term would see the Grammar School in situ in Tynedale Drive. That and the news that my sister was changing husbands and yet another good-looking fella would be living in our house in the near future to begin another round of screaming, shouting and fighting. And that final piece of information just about put the icing on the cake. Unfortunately for myself my star sign was Leo and therefore, whether one believes in the accuracy of astrology or otherwise I found it difficult to handle change. Perhaps my moon was in Uranus or something. Had it been just one change then I could perhaps have coped but with multiple changes in the offing they just threw my life out of kilter.

The move from Axwell would mean that all of our neighbours would be left behind. No more Weir, Watson and Thomson across the road. No more Brenda, Isobel, Walter and Nellie next door. No more Armstrong, Harris, Connor and Fowler just along the street from us... and no more Roly Forman... and that final name brings me to the one unexpected blip in the planning... one ill-advised slip of the tongue which I would come to regret.

"Where ye gannin' Jim?"

The voice came from behind me. I hadn't noticed Roly sitting on the low wall at the side of his house - 33 Axwell as I walked past to begin my adventure. "Hi Roly, didn't see ye there. I'm gannin campin' with the YM."

"No yer not," came the strident reply.

"Aye I am... we're gannin to Otterburn."

"Load of plop... Titch towld us man, yer runnin' away from yem agen." Roly was being really loud and I was immediately scared that his mam or dad would hear and put two and two together.

"Roly... shut up man. Naebody knows except Titch. I wish I hadn't told him now but I had to cos he lent me his dad's primus thingy."

"Titch has already told loads of people man... everybody knaas. They're even havin' bets aboot how long afore ye get caught. Anyways can aahh come wi' yer?" Roly wasn't being loud anymore and he seemed as if he was serious. I honestly didn't know what to do. If I said no then he could just open his clagger and blab to his mam and dad and before you knew it my plan would be destroyed before it even got off the ground. I could be nabbed before I got on the Newcastle bus. But if I said yes then I would be stuck with having to think for two people instead of just myself.

"Roly... aahhmm really runnin' away ye knaa... aah'm not kiddin'."

"Aye aahh knaa, but yer not the only one who's fed up. Wait a mo and aahll just get me jacket." He didn't give me time to say yes or no... but swung his legs over the wall and headed for the back door of 33 Axwell.

My stomach sank. I couldn't say no but knew that it was a huge mistake to even think about having Roly along. His planning was non-existent. 'Hang on and I'll get my jacket' didn't really cut it as serious plotting. I knew he'd have no money and no idea of the big plans that I had swirling around in my head. We'd discussed running away once before at the Miner's Welfare but hadn't followed through with it. Now it seemed he was doing it as a jolly. Something to fill in a few boring hours. I was conflicted but my options were limited. Say no and risk everything going belly up like my first attempt... say yes and drag Roly around with me and have to subsidise him. It was difficult but I chose the second option.

In retrospect I thought that maybe he'd tire of the idea and I could convince him to bail out and then give him his bus fare back from Newcastle. Perhaps then I could plead with him to give me at least a day start before he opened up his gob and blabbed to any adults. All these thoughts were swirling around in my head and I was immediately having to deal with problems. Up to that moment I hadn't foreseen any obstacles emerging... none whatsoever until my forthcoming attempt at avoiding the ticket inspector and dodging around on the train... but I'd planned for that.

Roly re-appeared from the back of his house shoving his arms into his jacket and smiling as he stepped over the low wall. "Howay then, let's away."

My gut was telling me that this was a big mistake but the deal had now been sealed and I couldn't do anything about it. The best I could do was to accept the situation and make a fist of it.

We talked as we walked to the bus stop on Cowpen Road.

"How much money have ye got Roly?"

"Half a dollar."

"A half croon... are ye kiddin' man? That's not enough."

"Aahh knaa, but ye can lend us some and aahll give it back to you when we get back yem tonight."

"Roly man... aahmm not comin' back tonight. Aahmm not comin' back ever."

"Yeh... that'll be right. Ye'll be back as soon as ye've lost aall yer dosh at the Spanish City."

"Aahmm not gannin to the Spanish City man. Aahmm headin' for the toon and Central Station."

Roly looked puzzled. "What ye gannin to Newcastle for?"

"To get a train doon ter London."

"Divvent be daft man that'll cost ye loads."

He was right of course in the general scheme of things but he didn't know about my master plan and as we waited at the bus stop I filled him in with all the detail. He looked incredibly impressed when I produced my bogus letter and let him know how the rest of the stratagem was meant to play out.

The bus came, a double decker. We got on and headed for the front seats upstairs. There followed a few minutes of silence during which I reckoned Roly must have been digesting the fact that this wasn't just another strop for a day. Inside his head the reality was beginning to bite. The realisation that this wasn't make-believe but a serious attempt to not only run away from home but also a determination to make it a permanent state of affairs gave him a jolt and he opened up.

"That letter thing is deed clever Jim."

"Aye... took us ages to get it right."

"Got any tabs?"

"Aye," I said as I rummaged in the side pocket of the rucksack and produced the packet of twenty cigarettes.

"Park Drive... where'd yer nick them from?"

"Aahh didn't nick them man, aahh bought them at that little tobacconist kiosk outside Blyth railway station."

"What did yer get them un's for?... they're cack."

I shrugged, "Divvent knaa... aahh just fancied a change. Anyways if they're cack yer'll not be wantin' one."

Roly laughed, "Divvent be daft... they're not as cack as Woodbines."

We took a tab each and sparked up then sat in silence for a few minutes... puffing away until we'd finished our smokes and ground the butts out on the floor of the bus.

It was Roly who ended the period of quiet. "Ye knaa that letter thing?"

"Aye what about it?"

He frowned as he answered, "Well it's just that aahh haven't got one... ye knaa... ter show the checky on the train when he comes aroond."

"That's not my fault man Roly. It took us ages ter plan it oot and mek sure it was brilliant. Ye cannit dee things like that at the last-minute man. Anyways this whole thing is stupid man... yer just feelin' bored so ye gan and put a jacket on ter run away from yem. Ye need to be proper serious man Roly and ye divvent need ter come if you're havin' second thoughts cos aahh can give ye the bus fare back ter Blyth."

By that time Roly was in apologetic mode, "No man aahh still want ter come with ye an' aahmm really serious. It'll teach me mam and dad a lesson aboot puttin' me pocket money up... ha-ha they'll probably give us ten bob a week when they find us in London. But Jim man what happens if aahh get nabbed by the checky?"

My heart sank... Roly still hadn't got his head around the 'never coming back' bit and he was with me just because he thought it was a jolly he could use to increase his pocket money.

"Roly man... aahmm not fannin' aboot and yer bein' a reet knob."

"No man Jim... listen, me dad got arrested on a train once... that was cos he didn't have a ticket. He'd had ower much ter drink and he got on the wrong train. He was supposed to be getting the Blyth train but he got on the London one by mistake and fell asleep. The checky got hold of him and locked him up. Me mam went crackers cos it cost us loads in fines and she didn't even knaa he'd been oot in Newcastle. Me dad got handcuffed in the guards van cos he had nee money and they kept him chained up until he got ter London and then the cops beat him up cos that's what they dee in London... and aah divvent want the same ter happen ter me."

"Knickers Roly... yer talkin' crap."

"Ask me dad then... but divvent let me mam know that I told you."

"Yah serious?"

"Course I am... that's why me dad never gans on the train anymore. He got his face squished in by a bunch of coppers in London... they're aall big buggers and they're aall just bouncers wi' uniforms on man."

Was Roly just making this up or was he telling the truth? don't ask why but I believed him. Those coppers didn't sound very inviting and a change of plan was needed to avoid them. My meticulously thought-out plan was beginning to unravel. Since Roly had become involved my straight line had become wonky and it felt like he had me cornered in my own head. It was time to improvise.

"So, ye don't want to go back to Blyth and ye don't want to gan on the train. What do you want to do then?"

"Think about it man Jim... what if the checky doesn't believe your letter? What if he captures me and makes me tell the truth? Not that aahh would say owt but what if they take me into the guard's van to torture me and make me tell... ye knaa? Like what if they start pullin' me fingernails oot or burnin' us wi tabs... aahmm canny brave like but those checkies knaa aall about the worst torture stuff."

The way Roly was telling it made the train idea seem less and less an attractive proposition but what was the alternative? We couldn't sneak onto a long-distance coach because they check your tickets before you even set off. We could probably go to North Shields and sneak on one of the ferries but then we'd end up in Norway or Holland and I didn't fancy that. I wouldn't have minded France though cos I knew how to ask for the toilet in French. 'Ou sont les bogs silver plate?'. My uncomplicated plan was becoming more complicated by the minute.

We arrived at the Haymarket, got off the bus and headed for Northumberland Street. My head was in a bit of a mess by this point and I didn't know what to do. Roly took the lead.

"Just askin' like but d'yer fancy gannin onto the Tyne Bridge and hitch-hiking?"

I'd run out of ideas and options so any suggestion was better than nothing. "Aye... fair enough but aahh divvent think that'll work. Naebody's gannin ter stop on the Tyne Bridge man."

"They will for me like."

"Aye cos you've got a magic thumb haven't ye?" I said sarcastically.

"Bet yer a quid that aahh get us a ride in half an hour."

"Roly man ye haven't got a quid ter bet with an' half an hour's too long ter be thumbin' on the bridge. We'll get noticed man."

"Okay then… bet yer a ha'f croon aahh get us a lift in ten minutes and anyway getting' noticed is the whole point isn't it?" He wasn't wrong.

A short walk later and we're on the Tyne Bridge. I'm sitting there minding my rucksack beside the barrier. Roly's taken the lead by this point and he's standing with his thumb out and two minutes after the first thumb a lorry pulls up and the window winds down. "Where ye heading for lads?" the driver shouted… and he looked friendly enough.

"London," shouts Roly.

"Are yiz runnin' away?" the driver asks.

"Aye," shouts Roly and I cringe.

"Hop in then… I'll take you as far as Doncaster."

We clambered into the lorry with Roly sitting closest to the driver and me next to the door with my rucksack. The lorry was an old one and smelt… well like an old lorry. On the dashboard was a framed photograph of the driver with his wife and a bunch of kids… there must have been at least half a dozen of them and ranging in age from about fifteen to a babe in arms. Hanging from his rear-view mirror was a Spanish lady doll in a red flamenco dress and on the dashboard in front of him was a Tupperware container piled high with sandwiches and biscuits.

As soon as we'd cleared the Tyne bridge and were motoring through Gateshead it felt like job done. Roly was a happy chap of course because he'd been proved right and now had an extra half-crown... cos a bet is a bet... and Doncaster here we come.

CHAPTER 9

Keep On Running

———————————————■———————————————

The lorry bloke was friendly enough and kept up a stream of conversation... mainly with Roly because I was too busy thinking out our next move and consulting my map. The driver's pile of sandwiches had dwindled away fairly rapidly and Roly had been complicit in their disappearance but I think the driver was feeling a little sorry for us. Roly had been spinning him a yarn about his wicked stepdad and his thick belt which he used to use on Roly when he came in from the pub. It sounded convincing... so I kept my head down and let Roly get on with it.

I kept my own counsel and watched the road signs as they flashed past. Washington, Durham, Bowburn, Bishop Middleham... and the miles kept ticking up. I could hardly keep my eyes open because I had been too excited to sleep last night and now fatigue was catching up. I thought I'd close my eyes just for a few seconds.

I can't remember falling asleep but I came to with a jolt as Roly dug me in the ribs with his elbow.

"Jim man... Derek wants ter knaa if we want a tea or coffee."

"Ehhh... what?"

"He's gone for a waz and then he's gannin ter have a cuppa in the café."

"What... when, where are we?"

"Leeming Bar man, ye've been fast asleep and fartin' and snorin' ya heed off. Howay let's get oot and hev a cuppa and a smoke cos Derek doesn't want any smokin' in his cab."

"Derek?"

"Aye man... ye knaa, the bloke who's givin' us a lift."

I opened the door and we both climbed down from the cab. I left the rucksack inside because my tabs by this time were in my jacket pocket. We both sparked up a cig and enjoyed the sudden rush of euphoria as we headed for the door of the transport café.

"Where's he gone Roly?"

"To the bog man for a waz."

"What if he tells someone that we're runnin away?"

"He won't dee that man. Aah've been tellin him a right crackin story like ye wouldn't believe. Give us another hour or two and aah'll hev him wantin to adopt us." He wasn't kidding either. Roly knew how to bend the truth and tell a tall tale... he was a master at it. We stood outside and finished off our tabs before walking into the transport café together.

"What are you lads having" asked the man doing the serving as we stood looking at the chalked menu on a board behind the counter.

The fare on offer seemed pretty sparse. There was an older bloke further back and he was turning sausages and eggs on a grimy hotplate. He was wearing a scruffy apron that looked as if it had been borrowed from a miner finishing a hard shift on the coal face. "Think I'll have a tea please," I said as Roly continued perusing the chalkboard.

"Aah'll hev a coffee please," said Roly, mind now made up.

"Black or white?"

"White," was his reply... Now, anyone of the younger generation reading this will probably find it difficult to understand that if you ordered a coffee in 1965 your choices were confined to 'black or white'. At those transport cafes there were no cappuccinos or lattes, no mocha or Irish, no fatty or skinny... no chocolate smiling face in your froth... no clever barista asking if you wanted spurgle-wurgle with tish-woosh or something equally silly. "Hold the tish my good man but heavy on the woosh." No, there was only coffee... out of a jar or a big catering tin and your choices were limited to black or white, with or without sugar. The milk would be in a glass jug and usually with a dead fly or two floating around on top while the sugar would be in an open bowl and not in little white or brown packets and generally there would be discoloured lumps in the sugar bowl where wet spoons had been thrust in and the sugar congealed.

I was feeling a little peckish but when I saw the sandwiches on offer I decided to give them a body swerve. I don't know how old those sandwiches were but some of them had decided to curl up and the edges of the ham poking out looked brown and as hard as nails. Anyway I had some Cornish pasties in my rucksack so I decided my cup of tea would suffice. So, a leisurely cuppa and a trip to the lav and soon we were on our way again. Derek was sitting waiting for us when we clambered back into the lorry.

"Hurry up lads, time's marchin' on and I'm behind schedule."

As we were pulling away a police car pulled up at the front of the building. Roly and I instinctively ducked down but Derek just laughed. "Them two coppers are never away from here. It's a wonder that they ever manage to catch any baddies. Don't worry lads they're not after you two... they're after a free cuppa and a bacon butty."

Then we hit the road and we took several diversions on our way to Doncaster as Derek made a few deliveries. Northallerton and Thirsk were next before we resumed our journey via Dishforth. Then came Boroughbridge, Wetherby and Knottingley before the longer stretch to Doncaster itself.

"I'll have to turf you out now lads," said Derek as we pulled into a side road just before hitting what we thought was Doncaster proper. "I'll get shot if my boss knows I've been giving lifts."

We accepted that and said our goodbyes after Derek pointed out the road we were to take for Doncaster and also the best direction for getting back to the main road for picking up another lift. For some reason he now seemed mighty keen to be shot of his two young runaways and within a matter of minutes his lorry was disappearing into the distance at speed.

"What was that aall aboot Roly?"

"Divvent knaa... he just changed. Wanted rid of us. He must have been nervous in case anybody saw him."

"Aye that's probably it... anyways we'd better get movin'... d'yer knaa what time it is?"

"No but it must be after tea-time. We've been on the road for ages."

"Derek said there was a shop that stays open late down that road. Are ye gonna buy a packet of tabs to keep us goin' until we get to London cos ye've been smokin mine aall day and aah've only got eight left?"

"Aye... aall right. But they might cost more here cos we're down south now man and they charge more for stuff."

"Roly man... London's down south not Doncaster. We're not even half way yet so we better get a move on. Tabs are probably cheaper here anyway."

Tabs turned out to be exactly the same price and Roly spent almost the whole of his five bob on a packet of twenty 'Escort'. We'd never tried those cigarettes before but they were cheap.

We set off walking but after about half an hour we suddenly realised there was no Doncaster in sight. We'd been dumped miles away and we were now walking through a place called Arksey. We were both fatigued with the excitement of the day. Roly was flagging as was I even though I'd had a sleep in the lorry.

"Where are we gannin to kip Jim?"

"Aahh don't know man Roly we'll just have ter keep on gannin."

"Howay man Jim aahmm knacked."

We were walking past a black and white timbered pub called the Plough Inn. It seemed busy which made me realise it must be well after seven o'clock. Then I had an idea.

"D'yer fancy goin' into the pub for some crisps and then askin' if there's anywhere around here that does cheap bed and breakfast? Aahll wait around outside for ye."

103

Roly didn't bat an eyelid "Aye okay but ye'll have ter give us some dosh cos aah've only got a tanner left from buyin' the tabs."

I had some silver and copper in my jacket pocket and I passed him a two-bob bit to pay for the crisps. He took it and headed for the pub. He had some real guts did Roly because he didn't think twice about it and I certainly didn't fancy walking into a crowded bar.

Five minutes later and Roly is standing in front of me. I'm sitting on the pavement with the contents of my rucksack scattered around me. I'm fourteen years old and close to tears because somehow my cash stash has gone missing. I've searched through every pocket and compartment at least twice... and the money has disappeared. My paper-lad money, my birthday presents money and my Parka cash... they're no longer in the side compartment of the rucksack where they were supposed to be. Twelve quid has gone walkabout.

I rant at Roly but pretty quickly come to realise that he hasn't taken the money and he's as gutted as I am because he's been given directions to a cheap bed and breakfast and he's obviously ready for some food and shuteye.

I've gone over the entire journey in my head and I know that the money was still tucked in that side pocket when we stopped at the café. I'd gone to take some money out before I realised I had almost a quid in change in my jacket pocket and the notes weren't needed.

Roly sat down beside me and handed me a bag of crisps. I tore mine open and began chomping... and I couldn't even be bothered to find the little blue bag of salt. Nothing would have tasted good just at that moment.

"Derek." One word from Roly and everything fell into place.

"Ehhh?"

"The driver man, he was back in the cab when we came back from the café. He must have nicked it."

The same thought had been swirling around in my head but there were a thousand other thoughts jostling for position. My normally clear-thinking brain was now a quagmire. "He wouldn't do that would he? somebody could have been hangin' around outside and sneaked up and taken it while we were inside havin' a cuppa man."

"Nah man... if it was somebody else they'd have just nicked off with the rucksack wouldn't they? They wouldn't take the time to go through all the pockets... so I reckon it must have been Derek cos he saw you goin' in that pocket a few times."

"Aye you're right and it probably was him but if it was there's nothing we can do about it. We can't go to the coppers."

"Why not... the bloke's a thief?"

"And say what... a bloke in a lorry nicked our runnin away money? Then they'll ask for our addresses and there's probably coppers already lookin' for us... we might even be on the telly by now man. Then we'll get handcuffed and put in a cell and we might even get bashed by the coppers like what happened to your dad."

Roly gave a sickly grin, "Aahh med that bit up... it never happened. Me dad never really got arrested or nowt... aahh was just tryin to mek ye think twice about jumpin' the train."

I couldn't bring myself to make a response to that. More fool me for being sucked in by a fairy story. If I'd had the courage of my convictions I could have been in London by now. I felt as if everything was falling apart and if I'd been able to bend down then run around and kick my own backside I would have done. We were out of options and I felt as low as I'd ever felt in my life. Then I looked up and suddenly remembered the battered car in the distance standing on some waste ground and minus tyres. I'd actually spotted it a while ago before I'd discovered the money was missing and hadn't given it a second thought. But now I had an idea.

"D'yer fancy kippin' in that car ower there until we can think of a plan?" That was the best I had to offer at that point.

"Jim aah'm hungry and tired man." Roly was at a low point too.

"Aah've got two pasties here and some Opal fruits."

"Righto but we can't live in a bliddy car man." The word pasties had made his mind up.

"Just until aah think of somethin' man. It'll keep us out of sight in case we're bein' hunted or owt."

Ten minutes later and we're huddled in the back seat of an old Morris Oxford. The front seats had been ripped out and the car was minus a dashboard. One of the doors was hanging off and there were only two windows which hadn't been smashed. But for a few hours it became our sanctuary as the evening moved on and the dark closed in.

We were both silent for a long time as the seriousness of our predicament began to sink in. We wolfed down the pasties and then had the Opal fruits for our pudding. When we lit up our tabs we crouched right down so that no passing stranger would see a suspicious glow from the old car. And August it may have been but it seemed mighty chilly in that decrepit motor.

From our den we saw the pub lights going out and a few raucous voices as a few inebriated punters left the pub and the odd car pulling away. That gave us a fair idea of the time. But it was chilly and we both realised that we couldn't stay there for the night. Apart from that although we'd warded off hunger pangs with the pasties we were both now thirsty. It was time to move on.

We were two depressed kids as we headed back to pick up the road we'd been on and then pointed ourselves in the direction we thought must be south. Roly was first to suggest a surrender. "We could go and hand ourselves in at a cop shop."

"No way," I wasn't having that. What a climbdown that would be.

"Then why not go to the nearest railway station and jump a train for Newcastle?"

"Roly man you're the one who talked me out of jumping a train for London with that story about your dad... and now ye want to do it?"

"Aye but that was then and this is now."

"What does that even mean?"

"Aahh don't know man but we can't keep on goin' to London with about ten bob left between us. It's stupid now man... let's just give up."

"Aahmm gonna keep goin Roly. It's up to you what you want to do. Anyway aahmm not makin' for London anymore... aahmm headin' for Luton. Me aunt Kitty and uncle Ronnie live there. And I've got a Cousin Shelley there an 'all.

"Is she bonny like?"

"Roly man she's only about eight or summat."

"Is she alright though?"

"Well... she did grass me up to mam for smokin' when we were down on holiday... but she's just a kid man. She thought it was funny."

"Right then let's start thumbin' at least we might get somewhere to sleep for a night."

Half an hour later and Roly's magic thumb had done the trick once again. This time it was a car he flagged down and we found ourselves in the company of a salesman on his way home from some sort of a conference. Roly sat in front engaging in conversation and pretending interest as the middle-aged man boasted about his latest sales victories in the double-glazing business. I was glad Roly was with me because he kept the bloke sweet as the miles ticked by.

I sat in the back seat and shared it with a sample case and wooden corner things with glass in that he must have used as demonstration pieces. I watched the road signs flashing by... Retford, Newark, Grantham and Stamford and I was just happy to be on the move again. Then after a while we pulled into a transport café and garage.

We were terribly thirsty and even though I was a little reticent about going inside just in case our pictures were on the telly or something I headed for the counter and I was just about to spend my final chunk of cash on a couple of teas, two sausage sandwiches and a bottle of pop when the double-glazing guy turned up behind me. "Okay son... I'll get them."

"Nah mister... it's all right." I protested.

"It's all right lad... I'll get them. I've just had the best week of sales in my entire life. Anyway, just call it a little present to help you on your way," and with that he just took over and paid for our order. I was seriously warming to the guy and when we found a table then sat and talked I realised that he was just a kind human being in a happy mood and there was no ulterior motive.

Then it was back on the road and I was doing my best to keep my eyes open as the towns flashed past... Peterborough, Huntingdon and Biggleswade. That final one gave me a jolt because I remembered Biggleswade being on road signs when I'd been on holiday to Luton recently.

"Can we stop soon mister?... I don't want to miss the turn off for Luton."

"I can't stop here lads but I can let you out at the next roundabout at Stevenage. That should be okay for you because you should be able to pick up a lift for Hitchin and then on to Luton. I'd take you myself but I'm off in the other direction to Harlow.

Ten minutes later and the man pulled his car to a stop on a big roundabout. "Get out quick lads... I'm not supposed to stop on a roundabout. If you walk over there under the flyover you'll see the signs for Hitchin. That's the road you need to get your next lift on. Best of luck lads and it's been nice meeting you. I hope your mam manages to leave that pig of a stepdad Roly... he needs someone to give him a good hiding... anyway got to go." And with that he was off and we were back out in the great big world again. I had to have a chuckle at Roly spinning the Charles Dickens abused orphan tale yet again but it had got us results. Who was I to complain.

A few minutes after the double-glazing bloke had dropped us off we headed for the roundabout exit that pointed us towards Hitchin. Suddenly a car came screeching around the roundabout and although we hadn't reached the Hitchin turnoff Roly stuck out his thumb. The car flashing past tooted repeatedly as it went by and we could see a bunch of blokes laughing and pulling faces. That didn't please Roly and he stuck two fingers up and began shouting "Cockney shitbags." That was a huge mistake.

Although the roundabout was big there were no other vehicles about at that time in the morning and we could see the car screeching around the perimeter and heading back towards us.

"Run Jim run," may sound like something out of a Tom Hanks movie but it was the very words that Roly shouted when we realised we were in a cauldron of trouble. We ran... oh boy did we run.

Who those guys were we didn't know and we never did find out but it scared the pants off both of us. We scrambled up a grassy bank as the car pulled up and the blokes jumped out... there were three of them... and they wanted blood. The bank was steep but we managed it in our panic and it led us into a farmers field of wheat, corn or something and we scrambled over a fence and then ran for our lives... we were truly scared. We ran like billy-oh.

We could hear the blokes shouting obscenities from the fence line but they didn't climb over and chase after us. I reckoned they must have been drunks coming back from a lock-in or a party but Roly thought they might have been plain clothes coppers. Whoever they'd been Roly and I had been really scared. We lay low in the field for ages afterwards and we didn't emerge until we'd heard the car depart and then gave it a further five minutes just in case. When we did surface light was just breaking so we thought it must be about five o'clock and as it had begun to drizzle we headed back for the roundabout and sat down under the flyover.

We were both exhausted, despondent and hungry and I was beginning to think that Roly's idea about handing ourselves in wasn't so bad after all. If the police had a nationwide hunt going on for us then it would mean they'd be aware that we might head for Uncle Ron and Aunt Kitty's house and if that was the case then we'd soon be captured anyway. So although Luton was only about an hour down the road that destination was now out of the question.

We sat down on the pavement and I took out the little primus stove and lit it for a touch of warmth. We both held our hands close to the heat, "Let's just have an hour's sleep and then we'll make a plan," I muttered as my eyes began to close. "I'll think of something." Roly didn't say a word.

CHAPTER 10

Homeward Bound

—————————————————————————————— ■ ——————————————————————————————

I don't know how long I'd been asleep but the honking of a lorry horn jerked me awake. It took me a long minute to get my head working and realise that I was sitting there on my own. The rucksack had vanished and so had Roly. Strangely enough I wasn't surprised... I was just disappointed. The primus stove was all that remained and it had burned itself out. There were no thought processes swirling around my head at that moment... my brain had deserted me and I must have sat there numb for a good ten minutes just staring as the occasional vehicle flashed past. I was running on empty and as head fuddles go this one must have been the world champion.

Then all sorts of rubbish began circulating around my brainbox. I was feeling sorry for myself and I began to think that moving on was pointless because no matter how far I travelled I would still have myself with me wherever I went. Maybe the problem was all of my own making because I seemed incapable of finding any kind of peace or happiness inside my own head so what would be the point in searching for it elsewhere. I was on a huge downer and I was completely on my own.

As it happened being on my own turned out to be good for me. I didn't have anyone else to worry about and that was a relief. Whatever plan or course of action I followed now it wouldn't need to be discussed, justified or defended. I was in total control.

I quickly exited my fogged-up state when suddenly in the distance I saw a police car. It was a good way off on an approach road when I spotted it and that gave me sufficient time to manoeuvre my backside out of there because I knew instinctively it was heading for me. I picked up the primus and headed up the same bank we'd climbed just hours before. I fumbled and dropped it and heard it roll away down the slope as I scrambled over the fence and I didn't have time to retrieve it. Then I made myself as small as possible in the wheat field... lying flat in a slight hollow... head down and breathing shallowly into the soil. I didn't know if Roly was in the police car but I was certain that he'd either gone and found the nearest cop-shop and gave himself up or had decided to hitch home on his own and had been picked up by the cops. I decided there and then that I wouldn't do the same and if I had to return to Blyth then I'd do it under my own steam and not with a police escort.

I heard the voices at the fence line. I wasn't sure whether one of the voices belonged to Roly. They were indistinct and I couldn't make out what they were saying so I lay in the field for a long time until the voices disappeared. I was hoping that the police wouldn't come up the bank with sniffer dogs to flush me out and hoped that I wouldn't hear the whirring rotors of helicopters hovering above me with searchlights and police marksmen with sniper rifles. I was overthinking it of course but hey... I was fourteen.

Then it began to rain and after a decent period of time and considering that it would now be safe I left the field. I couldn't find the primus as I negotiated the slippery downslope of the bank and presently I gave it up as a bad job. I made a mental note to avoid Titch for the foreseeable because it was his dad's primus stove. Then I began walking until I came to the slip road of the A1. There was a big sign which said, 'The North'. I did a Roly and began to use my thumb and within a matter of minutes I found that mine worked too.

My first lift was with a husband and wife and what a lovely couple they turned out to be. They were fantastic and friendly and for better or worse I opened up and found myself telling them my story... my true story and not a Roly cum Charles Dickens fiction. I found out during that part of my journey that nice people... caring people did exist and I'd been lucky enough to bump into these two. Mary and Alfred were their names and they were heading for their newly bought house in Richmond. They said they would take me as far as Scotch Corner and see what they could do about finding me a lift to take me on to Newcastle.

We made two stops on our journey north that day and on both occasions I was fed and watered by these two lovely people. I insisted on taking their names and address so that I could thank them properly when I'd got back home and able to do something to reimburse them for their kindness.

Mary wrote out all the details of their address together with a contact telephone number but they both insisted that they didn't want repaying. Alfred said that if his son was ever in a similar predicament then he hoped that someone would show him the same level of kindness. I really admired those two and I reciprocated and wrote out my address too. For a fair few years afterwards I would receive a Christmas card from Mary and Alfred Gaines. I do hope their lives were happy.

When we eventually arrived Scotch Corner turned out to be a big hotel and a filling station. It was the point at which the A66 branched off from the A1 to take traffic over towards the lake district and western Scotland while the A1 continued in a north-easterly direction to take traffic into Durham, Northumberland and eastern Scotland.

Parked up at Scotch Corner Mary and I sat talking in the car while Alfred set out on his mission to make sure I had a lift to take me north when they eventually left me. We sat chewing things over for ages about home and families, successes and disappointments, hopes and dreams and I let her know how appreciative I was of their efforts to help me and for the friendship they'd shown.

Mary said to me, "If you are lucky enough to find good friends make sure you hold on to them... because they are God's way of apologising to us for our families," then she laughed but it made me think. Then she said, "Jim this car journey at the moment is just a pointless passage in time but in years to come when you're older and wiser you'll cherish this memory." I remember those words often. She was correct then and correct ever since. It's a moment I'll never forget.

Alfred had been missing for half an hour or more on his mission but when he returned he seemed a happy bunny. He opened the car door, climbed into the driver's seat and turned around with a big grin on his face. "I've managed to get you a lift all the way to Gateshead. It's with a nice young fellow called Kevin who works in the hotel but you're going to have to wait until seven o'clock when his shift finishes... so you've got a few hours to kill."

Alfred handed me a pound note before we said our goodbyes. Just a little something to keep me going he said. Then they were gone and I have to admit to a sinking feeling in the pit of my stomach as I watched them drive away towards the A66. They'd been a lifesaver for me and now I was on my own again and I had those few hours to kill.

Guess what the first thing I bought with the quid was? Some tabs... what a surprise!

I sat around outside for those few hours. The rain had stopped so I sat and thought about all the happenings of the previous days. I kept close to the car that Alfred had pointed out to me as being Kevin's and I puffed away on my cigarettes... a packet of Players no less.

Kevin surfaced as expected not long after seven o'clock and introduced himself. He was okay as it happened but I did get the impression that Alfred must have pressured him into giving the lift. Just little remarks with hidden nuances made me think that he wasn't too happy about the current situation but that didn't stop him from sharing my cigarettes. I asked Kevin why he was working at Scotch Corner but living in Gateshead a zillion miles away but I don't remember him giving me a logical reply.

We set off and now I was watching the same road signs as I'd been clocking while travelling in the opposite direction just a short while before. Darlington, Newton Aycliffe and Durham came and went as our conversation in the car became more stilted as the minutes ticked by. When we came into Gateshead I don't think we'd talked for about half an hour and I was eager to abandon my latest lift. I think Kevin was equally as pleased to see the back of me and there were only a few pleasantries exchanged as we took leave of each other.

I'd been dropped off on Coatsworth Road and from there I just had to follow my instinct because my trusty map was somewhere on a journey in my missing rucksack. I was feeling so weary as I trudged along and I took several wrong turns before I finally reached the Tyne Bridge and stumbled my weary way back into Newcastle.

I didn't know what time it was but I was past caring by then and I headed for 'Bowers' the all-night café down beside Central Station. I was starving of hunger and thirsty too and I had enough money left over from Alfred's quid to invest in a bacon and egg sandwich and a cuppa. I didn't have a watch but the clock on the café wall told me it was almost midnight. I'd been thinking it was about ten o'clock. Where had all that time gone? It meant I was now stuck in Newcastle until the first bus for Blyth left the Haymarket in the morning.

I would have stayed in 'Bowers' eking out my remaining cash until it was bus time had it not been for the shifty looking bloke sitting by himself in the corner of the café. He was wearing what appeared to be an army greatcoat and his face sported two or three days of stubble. I tried to avoid his gaze as I sorted out a table because there was something spooky about him. I was aware he was watching me as I took my plate and sat down.

"Missed your bus bonny lad?" was the question as the shifty bloke limped over to my table after a few minutes and sat himself down opposite me.

"Aye," I forced out through a mouthful of sandwich.

"It's a bugger when that happens," the man grinned and I immediately noticed that one of his teeth was black.

"Aye," I forced out once again and I really wanted the bloke to go away so I could finish my sandwich in peace.

"I've been waiting for my nephew but he must have missed the train up from York. He's round about your age... fourteen, fifteen. He should have been here by now."

I didn't have a response to that. It wasn't a question. I carried on eating but his mere presence had taken some of the enjoyment out of the moment.

"So is it fourteen or fifteen?" he asked but with an edge to his voice which made me nervous.

"Seventeen," I lied.

"Aye that'll be right... and I'm a hundred and three."

This bloke was getting right up my nose so I thought a bit of cheek might be in order. "That's funny cos you look much older."

"Ohhh we've got a clever lad here have we?" he didn't seem best pleased and he was making me feel very uncomfortable.

"Gonna get some pop," I said then stood up and walked over to the counter. "Can aahh have a glass of orange please?"

The man took my money and served me but as he slid the glass of pop over he made eye contact and whispered. "Watch it son... shirt-lifter."

I didn't know what he meant but it sounded ominous and I knew that he was referring to the interloper at my table because there wasn't anyone else about.

I turned around and headed back with my pop but picked another table and sat myself down. The man who stole shirts wasn't impressed.

"Not good enough for ye now lad? Think yer better than me d'yer?"

I didn't reply but kept my head down and concentrated on my pop and lighting up a tab.

"Hoy us one of them ower. Aahmm oot of smokes but aah'll give ye one back when we get ter mine."

"Ehhh?"

"Ye can kip at my hoose... on the couch like. It's not ower far maybe ten minutes... just off Westgate Road. Give us one of them tabs and we can start walkin' ower in a bit man."

Black tooth was really scaring me now and the penny had dropped. I suddenly realised what the serving guy had meant by 'shirt-lifter'.

I quickly decided on my next course of action. This bloke had me marked down as prey and I didn't fancy that starring role. His table was between me and the door so my next move had to be convincing. I was shaking like a jelly because he was one hefty lump but I had noticed earlier that he walked with a limp so my quickly thought up plan had a good chance of success.

119

I stood up and picked up my glass, "Aye right, aah'll just fetch me pop ower. aah've only got Players... are they all right for ye?"

Black tooth must have thought all his birthdays had come at once. He gave a big smile and it wasn't a pretty sight. "Aye they'll dee."

I made on as if I was taking the tab packet out of my pocket as I plonked the glass of pop on the table and then clumsily knocked it over. The orange juice splashed over black tooth's trousers and as it did I made a spurt for the door as he began to curse and jump back from his seat. He was still turning round and rubbing at his pants as I ran out of the café and boy did I run like the wind. I didn't hear any sounds of pursuit but there again I didn't turn around to look, not even once and I kept running until out of breath.

I eventually found myself in Grey Street. It was well-lit and I slowed down because there were a few people about. They were mostly drunk I reckoned and must have been to a local club or something but they didn't pose any threat to me... just a bunch of blokes having a good time and professing undying affection for each other.

I carried on walking with the occasional glance behind to make sure I wasn't being stalked by black-tooth and half an hour later my thumb did the trick once again as I navigated my way out of the town centre following the number 6 bus route. I thumbed down a lift somewhere beside Exhibition Park.

A Triumph Herald pulled up in front of me with a squeal of brakes. The guy who picked me up was as drunk as a monkey and could barely string consecutive words together but he drove almost perfectly. He accepted a tab from me when I offered but our conversation was virtually non-existent apart from his opening, "Wind your window doon for the smoke... me wife doesn't like it. Tek ye as far as Klondyke."

Klondyke suited me fine because it was just a couple of hours walk from there into Blyth but now with the end in sight I was as nervous as anything.

God must have had himself a night on the beer that evening because it was peeing down from the heavens when I got out of the car, thanked the driver and began walking through High Pit. Within minutes every single inch of my clothing was dripping wet and the only dry bit was my hair under the plastic bag on my head.

That walk was the loneliest of my life... from High Pit down to Shankhouse then on to Bog Houses. Next came a detour from the main road... past the Three Horse Shoes pub and into the wilderness. I don't know why I chose that route but my trundle down the Hathery Lonnen was really spooky. For the whole distance I seemed to be followed by an angry owl and I could hear things moving about in the undergrowth and I knew it wasn't courting couples. That part of the walk felt endless but eventually with a huge dollop of relief I left the Hathery behind. Back to the main road and civilization then on past the Bebside Inn... through Bebside proper and onto Tynedale. The rain hadn't let up at all in fact it was getting heavier and more depressing. And the closer I came to Axwell the more terrified I became. My backside felt like it was chewing a lump of toffee. I almost turned around to begin another escape attempt as I passed the Red House and climbed the Axwell bank. I thought I may be in for a good hiding.

There were no lights on in any sitting rooms apart from the one at my house... 29 Axwell. The curtains were drawn but I could see shadows moving around behind them. I walked past the house and found myself heading for the railway line... I don't know why. I must have stood at the side of the Falloon house for a good fifteen minutes. I was terrified. I managed to light up a tab because I'd kept the important things dry and I indulged myself with the condemned man's final smoke before the black bag over the head and the rope around the neck. In my head a Catholic priest was squawking some gloomy passage from the bible just before the lever was pulled. I puffed away until the tab end began to burn my fingers. Drawing in a deep breath I headed for my date with destiny.

I finally made it to our front door and I could hear voices from inside as I stood under the concrete canopy with my hand hovering... afraid to knock but knowing I had no choice.

Then I gathered together all my scraps of brave and did it... 'knock-knock-knock' and prepared for the storm.

CHAPTER 11

Don't Let Me Be Misunderstood

———————————■———————————

I needn't have worried. The expected interrogation and grilling never materialized. On the flip side there were no greetings or sighs of relief, no cuddles or other expressions of affection. Those type of things were what daft French folk did and they were anathema in our house.

I hadn't been inside the door more than a few minutes when I was packed off to have a hot bath and then ushered to bed. There hadn't been a single question as to why I'd run away from home. Not a single question as to where I'd been or how I was feeling or even why I'd come back. I found the whole lack of questions to be deeply disturbing.

My bed had never felt so welcoming and I slept for the remainder of that early morning and for the rest of the day and when I finally surfaced at breakfast time the following day there wasn't a single reference to my running off escapade. It was as if it had never taken place but it wasn't surprising because that's how our family dealt with problems... they were swept under the carpet and their existence strenuously denied.

Apart from being told to keep away from Roly Forman because he was a bad influence and being asked as to my destination every time I went out on my bike there wasn't any further mention about those three days other than a comment from my mother about the guy Errol Davies who ran the YMCA. She called him a scruffy weirdo. Other than that you would think that those three days hadn't happened. Now would begin the Bates family subterfuge and shift any blame for the incident onto someone else. It wasn't fair and it wasn't right but it's just how our family operated. Also I was disappointed because mam had washed my jeans and inside the back pocket had been the address and phone number of Mary and Alfred Gaines and the paper was now completely destroyed.

That fact would haunt me for a number of years because of the Christmas cards they sent me but I couldn't return the compliment. They never repeated their address and it always made me feel awful that I couldn't respond in kind. I did try to track them down but to no avail. I hope those kind folk didn't think I'd forgotten them.

All the other kids in the street knew that I'd been on my travels and for a good few days I was the local celebrity. Irene Weir the lass from across the street couldn't stop asking questions about London and what it was like and had I seen any band members of the Beatles or Manfred Mann. I didn't have the heart to let Irene down and admit that I'd bottled out about fifty miles before London proper. I told her that I thought I'd seen Paul Jones in one of the Soho pubs but I couldn't go in to check because I was too young. I thought he'd been having a pint with Freddie Garrity and one of the blokes from Billy J Kramer and the Dakotas but I couldn't get near enough to be sure. That lie gave me kudos and for a while I happily lapped up the fame. It was Roly who eventually had my story shot down in flames when he told everyone the truth... aye Roly... grrr.

I never did get to find out what had happened to the rucksack because it turned up after a few days... returned by a policeman and it was never mentioned again. Also I didn't know how Roly had managed to get home because he'd made it back the day before me. I didn't know whether he'd thumbed home or been picked up by the cops and shipped off under escort. I'm sure he'll tell me if he reads this and decides to correct some of the details. I heard whispers of course but at the time as our two families were now not on speaking terms I couldn't manage to get to the truth of it.

My second day of being home and I was roped into helping to carry buckets of coal next door to the Nichol family coalhouse. I worked away with Walter and one of his sisters... it may have been Isobel or Brenda and we were transporting the half load of coal that my dad sold to our next-door neighbours. It was one of the perks of working at the pit... too much coal was delivered for one family so you could make a few bob extra by selling on the surplus. Even so there wasn't any mention of my latest escapade and it was beginning to worry me. Either Walter and his sister didn't know anything or they were studiously avoiding the subject. Maybe I'd just imagined the whole thing... it certainly felt like it.

It would be a week or so later before anyone actually turned around and named my escapade for what it had been... a failure. And of course it would be Tug and his old chums who would hang a label onto the event that dared not speak its name... especially if my mam was listening.

I headed for Tug's house on the Sunday following my return from the London attempt. I was pretty confident that news of my runaway fiasco wouldn't have filtered as far as New Deleval and I certainly wasn't about to mention it. Things on the home front were slowly returning to a sort of normalcy and I was happy to let the whole charade ebb away and become an event that I could put down to an unhappy experience.

Neither Tug nor his dog Winston were in the house when I knocked. I checked by peering through the windows but everything was as expected. The house was all neat and tidy and locked up. There were no evening papers on a Sunday so I reckoned I knew where Tug would be. He'd have strolled up the lonnen towards Horton farm because about a half mile down that beaten up old wagonway there was a rickety wooden bench and the old fogeys would meet up there on a regular basis to sort out the problems of the world without women present. So that's where I headed.

Sure enough the three old gadgies were deep in conversation when I finally spied them and pulled up on my bike. The trio were... Tug in an old brown jacket with ever faithful Winston at his feet, an old fellow called Mordy with a flat cap and a long old clay pipe which always smelled as if he was smoking festering turnips... and finally a dapper old man with a nice overcoat and a black dog with only one eye and a damaged ear. The dog was named Biscuit and lay obediently at his feet snuggled up beside Winston. The dapper man's name was Taps Bob although I'd never delved too deeply into why.

"Hi Tug, hi Mordy, hi Taps." I regretted that immediately when I saw the angry look on Tap's face and realised that the name might only be used by close friends and I certainly wasn't one of those.

The response to my greetings were muted to say the least and I had the feeling that maybe I was intruding. Perhaps they were talking old folk stuff and they didn't need a youngster volunteering his opinion. No-one spoke for a few seconds and I was feeling very self-conscious... then Tug cleared his throat and ended the impasse.

"Hell of a lang way for you to be bikin' Jimmy. Your legs must be canny tired by now."

That was a strange opening, "Ehhh... what ye on aboot? It doesn't tek lang from Cowpen."

"Cowpen?... aahh right I understand noo. Aahh thowt ye must've pedalled aall the way from London."

So they had heard. News of my escapade had indeed filtered through to New Deleval and from the opening tone of the conversation I quickly realised I wasn't flavour of the month.

I gave them a weak smile. "Aye so ye've all heard. Aahh didn't think that news would have got ower here man. The London attempt thing was a bit disappointing."

"Disappointing... a bit disappointing is that what ye want ter caall it?" said Mordy with a questioning frown.

"Aye... of course it was."

"Haddaway man... ye should call it what it was Jimmy... it was nowt else but failure... plain and simple."

"Failure, what are ye on aboot?"

Mordy didn't hold back. "Aahmm on aboot yersell Jimmy. Shankin' off ter London and then gannin flaky and giving up isn't disappointin' it's full-on failure man. Ye wouldn't even be here if you'd been successful... but callin' it disappointin' man... that's a laugh and a half." He held his hand up to deflect any interruption before continuing, "Sittin' doon on Blyth beach with an ice-cream and the top bit falls off and you're left just holdin' the cornet... that's what disappointin' is man."

Taps Bob decided to put his two-pennorth in, "Aye that's right what Mordy's sayin'... and another thing, hev ye ivvor sat on the netty and had a crackin' shite then fund the bog roll isn't there... just the cardboard bit in the middle and ye've got ter scrape yer arse wi that? that's disappointing."

Tug was laughing out loud at that one but still pulled his pal up, "Howay Bob man," he chuckled, "there's nee need ter be crude."

"Aahh knaa man... but disappointing? Failure is failure and nowt else. Disappointment is what happens when ordinary things gan wrang when yer not expectin' them. Not packin' in like Jimmy's done cos things got a bit tough. If us lot had done that against the Jarmins we'd nivvor have won the war. We've aall been through bad stuff and carried on anyway. There must have been plenty disappointment in your life Tug?"

Tug needed a long think to come up with an answer but when he did it shut everyone up. "Sittin' in me back garden a few weeks ago with nee shirt on cos it was a scorcher and aahh needed some sunscreen on me back. Then aahh remembered that Ethel wasn't aroond ter dee it for us anymore... noo that was really disappointin'... and made me feel very lonely."

All eyes were fixed on the ground as a response to Tug's comment. No words were exchanged and the silence seemed very loud.

"Howay sit yersell doon Jimmy. We've had wor say and that's that." Tug broke the silence and patted the bench beside him.

I sat down but said, "I'm feelin pretty stupid just now you lot."

Following Tug's reaction there was a murmur of sympathetic understanding from the oldies and then Mordy spoke up, "Aahh Jimmy man tek nee notice of us cos there's plenty folk even stupider than you," he said by way of a backhanded apology.

"Sartinly is," said Tug... now feeling guilty after the three-pronged attack on me and smiling again after the sad remembrance of his wife, "Worraboot thon daft bloke up the top of the Oval who was lying in bed fixin' his bike while his wife was lyin' next to him havin a bairn. He was lucky the midwife didn't punch his lights oot."

That started a round of laughter. "Aye... ye'll nivvor be that stupid Jimmy," said Taps Bob, "That bloke has just aboot enough intelligence to open his mouth when he wants to eat, but sartinly nee more."

More laughter followed and the mood had changed.

"Anyways kid... d'yer happen ter have a pair of tweezers on ye? Mordy's gone an' got a spelk in his thumb off the bench," asked Taps Bob. "Divvent want ter be diggin' it oot wi' a penknife."

"Me? a pair of tweezers? aahmm not a lass man." That reply caused a few chuckles.

"Jimmy here have a tab," said Tug and offered a packet of Players Weights. I didn't refuse and didn't make any cheeky seeking the doctor comment on this occasion. I took a cigarette out of the proffered packet and sparked it up. I'd never smoked one of these before.

"Ta Tug... I'm out of smokes myself apart from a couple of nippers."

"Short of cash now are ye... with nee paper job?"

"Aye summat like that Tug."

"That's how we found out aboot ye runnin' away man. Yon Joe lad who took ower your roond told us."

"Ohhh aye... of course. Aahh never thought about that."

"Anyways Jimmy are ye gannin to tell us what went on and why it went doon the pan?... but the truth mind... like it actually happened." Tug was being serious. They really wanted to know the ins and outs of the whole episode and why it had finally failed.

So I launched into my story and spent the next half hour giving the three stooges a blow-by-blow account of my recent escapade and I left nothing out. They sat silently for the most part with just the occasional interruption and as I talked I realised that I was brightening up their day. A mundane few hours talking about leeks or allotments had morphed into an adventure story with myself in the screen hero role and I didn't hold back on the detail. When I came to the end of the tale and finished with the part about my recapture or indeed my surrender my story tailed off and there was a studied silence.

Three old blokes sat puffing on their chosen stimulants of bliss. They smoked silently, thinking about the tale they'd just been told. I watched them and smoked another of Tug's tabs and wondered how Mordy managed to keep that old clay pipe alight and how he managed to stand the disgusting smell. Taps Bob puffed elegantly on a long brown cheroot and Tug smoked two of his Weights... lighting the second from the glowing butt of the first before another word was spoken. Whatever I'd told them seemed to have given up much food for thought.

Tug was first to speak as he finished tab two and ground it underfoot.

"Jimmy... what did aahh tell ye aboot getting' other folk involved. Too many cooks spoil the broth man and there's truth in that owld sayin'. On yer tod ye can mek aall yer own decisions and be master of your own destiny. As soon as there's two involved then you give up independence for the sake of company and it nivvor ends well."

"Aye but to be fair Tug Jimmy gave it a decent crack," chipped in Mordy with his pipe now extinguished. "It wasn't just a coward job after aall... so divvent be ower hard on him. He had a choice to make and chose wrong... and we've aall done that man Tug."

"Aye yer right... aahh knaa that. The big lie and the plannin' was impressive and the letter thing was bliddy good an' all... crackin' in fact. It was me that told Jimmy that if ye ever tell a lie mek sure it's a big'un cos little lies always get found out. That's reet isn't it Jimmy?... aah told ye ter lie big like Hitler or Goebbels or one of wor politicians."

"Aye Tug ye did."

"Aahh just got a bit disappointed when I heard ye hadn't made it ye knaa... with me son bein doon in London playin with one of them daft bands. Aahh hoped maybe... aahh I don't know what I hoped." He didn't say anything else for a while as he and Mordy began a silent fishing practice routine. It was weird. Mordy was pretending to cast a line and Tug was pretending to reel in a fish. They were chuckling away and obviously enjoying the moment.

But Tug with a son in London? That was a bolt from the blue so I interrupted their fishing practice. "I didn't know you had a son Tug. What's he doing down in London and what band is he in? He must play in one of the old-time big bands or something like Joe Loss cos he must be canny old."

"Tug had three sons," Taps Bob chipped in, "But two of them never made it home from the war."

"Heroes they were... heroes," said Mordy then quickly shut up.

"Aahh divvent knaa aboot that," Tug smiled awkwardly, "but I hope they did their bit... cos they'll nivvor be forgotten man. Them not mekkin' it back yem nearly finished wor lass." Then there was a long pause.

"The youngest son... he's called William and he was my mistake. Not that aahh mean a proper mistake. It's just that I was in my forties when he came alang. A huge surprise he was cos the war was brewin' and me and Ethel had said nee mair bairns. We were both gettin' ower old for nippers ye knaa but William came alang anyway three years afore the war. He must be nearly thirty noo man."

"So do you not see him?" I asked... almost apologetically.

Tug looked saddened and sat for a few seconds with shoulders hunched before replying, "Nah he left home at fifteen and went doon London ter live with one of Ethel's relatives and he started usin' Ethel's maiden name... Perks. That was a kick in the teeth when he stopped usin' Stevenson. Ethel knew how upset aahh was. She would have gone spare if she knew what he's doin' for a livin' now man... playin' a bliddy guitar."

"A guitar?"

"Aye... in one of them groups what the kids like. Ye knaa wi' lang girly hair and stupid clothes. The thing is he changed his name agen and noo he calls hisell Wyman or summat. Man he's ower owld for aall that kid stuff... he should be deein a proper job... but it's his life aahh suppose."

I was feeling a bit sad for Tug but at the same time I was intrigued with this latest nugget of information. Surely Tug's son couldn't be....

"Bill Wyman Tug? Are you sayin' his name now is Bill Wyman?"

"Bliddy right man... Bill Wyman indeed. He gans on stage with a bunch of monkeys called the Boolin' Stones or summat. And the idiot that does the singin' cos he cannit play nee instruments is some ugly chimp of a kid called... ohhh what's his name agen... aye Mark Jiggler... aahh think."

I couldn't believe what I was hearing, "Could it be the Rolling Stones and Mick Jagger? Cos if it is that ugly chimp of a kid has the most beautiful lass in the universe... Marianne Faithful for his girlfriend."

"Aye that could be it... the Rolly Stones. Aahh heard them on the wireless man not lang ago singin a song they'd pinched off another bloke called Buddy Holly cos they cannit even sing their own songs. But Jimmy ye must promise not ter tell naebody aboot me son and what a failure he is cos aahh tell everybody that he's a bricky doon London."

Tug was completely unaware of how successful his son actually was. The Stones were huge and Bill Wyman... Perks... Stevenson must be rolling in money. The Rolling Stones were certainly rolling in girlfriends according to 'Rave' and 'NME'. I began to look at Tug with new eyes.

"Tug I won't say a word," I promised... knowing full well that it was a secret that was just unkeepable.

"Aye... well mek sure ye don't. Anyways aahmm gannin yem noo to feed the hens... d'yer want to come?"

I did of course because Tug had tabs and I didn't. In short order we took our leave of Mordy and Taps Bob and they were really very pleasant. My supposed failure had now been consigned to history.

CHAPTER 12

The Last Time

Although I didn't know it that day was to be the last time I ever saw Tug. But it was a good day.

We said very little on the walk back down the lonnen. I was pushing my bike although I had offered Tug a crossbar because he was struggling with his walking... and he'd laughed. "And whereabouts are ye gannin ter put Winston when aah'mm gettin' me croggy? Cos divvent be fooled by the quiet nature Jimmy... my Winston would hev ye for breakfast if he thowt ye were tekkin us away." Somehow I didn't doubt his words.

We worked together in the back garden that day. Very little was said as we grafted in tandem... feeding the hens, doing the final earthing up of two rows of taties and checking a raised bed of carrots for any sign of carrot root fly. Those little buggers had managed to infest Tug's parsnips on ground level but not the raised carrot bed. I learned that day that those pests cannot fly up above two to three feet and that slice of information was stored away to be used to great effect in later years.

Tug and I carried a pouffe and a ladder-back chair into the garden and sat there in the warmth of the afternoon sun after our labours. We sat for quite a while without much conversation. For whatever reason Tug was handing out smokes like they were going out of fashion... and I didn't complain but it did make me wonder why.

There was very little outside noise that day. It was pleasant and peaceful. After a while just relaxing and smoking and enjoying the moment we began to talk.

I spoke up first because the side of Tug's face was all bruised and looked quite painful yet he'd never mentioned anything. I'd first noticed the purple discolouration up the lonnen but neither Mordy nor Taps Bob had made any reference to the bruising.

"So what's with the bruises Tug?"

"Ohhh them buggers," he said as he ran his fingers over the affected area, "aahh was doon here the other day hoyin' pellets and stuff aboot and bugger me if aahh didn't trip ower and smack me face on a chicken."

He was making light of the situation but he seemed uncomfortable and moved the conversation on quickly, "Ye knaa Jimmy that Taps and Mordy weren't havin' a go at you personally when they were mouthin' off. They're old school fellas like myself who came through the first war. A canny few of our old pals never came back from France but they went out there and did their duty until the bitter end. They were just a bit disappointed that ye'd given up."

"I know Tug... but at the time I didn't seem to have an option."

"You've always got an option Jimmy. Always got a choice."

"I'll do better next time Tug. Anyhow I wasn't that bothered about runnin' away... not really."

"Noo that sounds like a 'nivvor fancied her anyway' excuse when some lass has just turned ye doon for a date. Divvent bother with any next times Jimmy. Ye've had two cracks at it and if ye keep gannin at the same thing ower and ower it'll drive ye daft man. Crack on wi' yer life and mek a good fist of it." Then he sat for a minute in silence drawing on his tab and staring away into the distance before continuing.

"Can ye mind what aahh said aboot a magic moment in yer life? When somethin' happens to turn yer whole world upside down?"

"Aye."

"Then just get on wi' livin' and gannin ter school and then startin' work cos a day will come when your life gets turned on its heed and ye'll look back one day and realise that was a moment that changed yer life."

"Like what?"

"Aahh divvent knaa man Jimmy it's different things for different folks. Aahmm not one of them Gipsy wimmen wi' a crystal ball."

"Okay, but what happened in your life Tug that changed everything for ye? When did ye know it had happened?"

Tug paused for a second then stood up slowly from his chair. He pushed his hands into the small of his back and gave a grunt as he stretched himself. I thought at first that he was going to ignore the question but he seemed to be jiggling thoughts around in his head. He pushed his shoulders back and threw his arms out to the side giving another grunt as he did so then. "Bliddy rheumatiz... pain in the bliddy backside," then he laughed, "And the hips and the knees and the ankles... flamin' thing."

"Are ye aall right Tug?"

"Aye Jimmy just owld and stiff and at the arse-end of life," said Tug then lapsed into another silence as he sat himself down again.

Maybe my question had been a bridge too far so I tried to change the direction of conversation, "Tug why did Taps Bob look like he was going to brain me when I used his name earlier?"

Tug chuckled, "Aye aahh was a bit consarned aboot yer safety when ye opened yer mooth. Nivvor call him Taps agen cos that's only for his owld marras like me and Mordy."

"Why's that... is it not just because he was a plumber or somethin' Tug?"

"Ha-ha, if only Jimmy. No it's because a lang time ago when we were aall at school together he got the strap for spellin' a word wrong. I can't remember what word but we had a monster of a teacher... a big ugly sod wi' a Kitchener moustache and that bugger took great pleasure in battering kids when they made a mistake. But ye couldn't tell yer mam or dad cos they thought that teachers were a class above us and beyond reproach from poor folk like us so ye just took yer beatin' and accepted that it was just the way the world worked." Tug stopped there before asking.

"D'yer knaa what an acronym is Jimmy?"

"Aye it's like putting letters for words... like YMCA and NHS."

"Correct... so the teacher gave Bob the strap and then told him that he was as thick as pig shit. Hence the TAPS."

"Aahh right I get it."

"Aye well forget it cos it's only a select few who can use that and we use it cos we knaa it's not true. Bob's the only one of us that ended up wi' his own business and bought his own house. Bob is our success story and we use TAPS to remind him where he once came from."

"Okay Tug... it'll never cross my lips agen."

"Aye it will Jimmy cos ye'll not be able to resist but mek sure that Bob nivvor hears it. Anyways ye were askin' aboot moments that changed me life so aall tell ye aboot the two that sticks in my mind the best."

"Ye mean ye can have more than one?"

"Aahh divvent knaa how many other folk have Jimmy. Some folks might only have one and some might have lots but aall tell ye aboot the two times that stick in my mind if ye'll just give yer mooth a bit of a holiday."

That shut me up and I didn't reply as Tug took two tabs out of his packet and passed me one. We sparked up and sat quietly for the first few puffs. Then Tug began.

"One of me moments changed me whole life and one of me moments changed the way that aahh view the world, but just give us a sec cos aahmm needin' the netty." With that Tug eased himself up and shuffled away into the house. He was away for a long time but when he came back he had two bottles of beer 'Double Maxim' and he used an opener to take the top off the first bottle before handing it to me. "Ever had a beer before Jimmy?"

"Aye of course... aahmm fourteen man."

"And whereabouts did yer have yer beer?"

"The Seven Stars ower North Blyth."

"Now why doesn't that surprise me?" He uncapped his own bottle and took a swig from it. He hadn't bothered to bring glasses. I joined him in the swigging. My mother would have gone spare if she could have seen me smoking and drinking... and Tug would have been mincemeat but I was feeling very grown up and I settled into the atmosphere as he began his tale.

"Me oldest lad was in hospital in Catterick. It was 1945 and he'd been wounded in Germany mevvys a week afore the war ended. He was in a bad way, really bad and he was pumped full of morphine. Either me or Ethel sat beside him for weeks but we couldn't get any sense oot of him... he was delirious and talkin' gibberish most of the time. Anyways the doctors pulled me aside one day and said they would have to tek both legs off above the knee otherwise gangrene would set in and finish him off." With that Tug fell silent for a long time and I didn't butt in. I sat silently with him because I could tell that he was struggling with the remembering of it. I felt for him.

Apart from the clucking of the hens as they foraged away in their play garden and the occasional sound of a car somewhere in the distance there was a stillness all around. Tug took a few minutes to compose himself and get his head around what he was about to say... then he continued and there were tears in his eyes as he spoke.

"God forgive us Jimmy but aahh prayed that me own son would just gan quietly in his sleep." Tug wiped at his eyes with the sleeve of his jumper. He took a swig from his beer bottle and then took two more tabs out of his packet. He handed one to me and we both lit up even though we'd just put the last ones out. I felt privileged to be made privy to Tug's inner thoughts but also incapable of understanding the depth of the turmoil he was going through.

"He was a canny footballer ye knaa... afore the war. He played for Shankhouse on the right wing and as fast as a whippet. Shankhouse had a good team then and he loved it... he even turned Spartans doon when they came knockin for him. Newcastle had been to watch him a few times an' all and aahh went to watch him whenever I could. Aahh thought mevvys he could have made it ye knaa... professional like. Aye but then Hitler went into Poland and it aall kicked off."

I kept my silence as I smoked because I just didn't have any words to add. It was much too big and personal for a fourteen-year-old lad to do anything but sit there and listen.

"Anyways... without gannin in ter aall the bad stuff and the heartache that nearly finished wor lass off... cos she was nivvor the same agen even though we avoided talkin' about it. Aye... it was bad for me and aahh mean really bad. But wor lass was a changed woman when that was aall ower. That lad of wors had come oot of her body Jimmy... so grief was different for her... ye knaa... more personal. A mother grieving and watchin' her bairn's life slippin' away. It was awful to see."

Tug stopped there and eased himself up without speaking. He made for the hens' play garden to usher them back into their coop. I didn't follow or offer any help. It seemed like the right course of action and I reckoned Tug needed some time alone in his head to gather his memories together. After a few minutes with the hens safely corralled he returned and sat himself down.

He began straight away, "The day wor Arthur died ye would have thought nowt was the matter. Ethel wasn't there. She had the young'un ter see to and she never forgave herself for not seein' Arthur off. But that day Arthur just came alive... for an hour ye'd have thought he was on the mend and he'd pull through. He was rememberin' stuff from his childhood. He was playin' football agen and courtin' lasses and workin' at the pit with aall his mates. He was playin' pitch and toss and havin' a tanner on the horses with Mordy's father... wor illegal bookie. He was havin' Christmas dinner and remembering one in particular when aahh told him it was his turn to kill one of the hens. Then he was laughing because he couldn't do it and he'd left it to me otherwise there'd have been nowt to eat apart from taties and gravy and sprouts and stuff. But then he got serious Jimmy... an' aahh mean proper serious." Tug paused there and sat deep in thought for a minute.

"He told me about the day he was wounded. My laddie Arthur was cryin' by this time with the memory. Not about getting wounded but aboot hoyin' a grenade at a German position then jumpin' into their trench and sprayin' bullets aall aroond. He thought they were aall deed but then he heard a noise behind him and he turned aroond and seen a soldier liftin his rifle up. He shot the Jarmin and killed him but when he went to check and mek sure he was deed it nearly finished him. The Jarmin was just a little lad, mevvys twelve- or thirteen-years-old. Arthur told me that he couldn't move. He'd just killed a bairn... a little bairn and even though his sergeant was shoutin' at him to get down he just stood there staring at the lad and thinkin' aboot his own mam and the German lad's mam."

Tug paused, deep in thought before continuing. "Anyway that's the last thing he could remember aboot that day cos a shell went off where he was standin'. But that day in that hospital my laddie Arthur was bubblin' his eyes oot and he said somethin' then that I'll never forget. He said, 'Ye knaa dad... when you take another life you don't get away scot-free because something important dies inside of you'. Then he said somethin' like, 'it meks ye wonder aboot the folk that run the countries... the rich folk... the entitled folk who've gone to Eton... the politicians and the clivvor folk that start aall these troubles. How clivvor are they... those rich folk who sit behind their desks and talk aboot war but it's not their rich pals they send to the front. It's the poor folk that they send to die for their incompetence. I despise them aall'.

"He died soon after that Jimmy, and I was holdin' his hand when he moved ower to the other side. But it was one of them turnin' points that aahh was on aboot. Because from that moment aahh stopped doffin' me hat to folk that wear collars and ties. Them teachers at your school are a case in point... folk that think they deserve respect cos they dress smart and taalk clivvor. And then aahh stopped voting an' all cos them Liberals, Labour and Conservatives they're aall in it for themselves... the privileged classes. They're aall worse than muck but aahh still think them Conservatives are the worst of the lot. Show me one of them fellas that says he's done an honest day's work in his life and I'll show ye a bliddy liar."

With that Tug stood up and went into the house without another word. I didn't follow because this was Tug's day in the sun... not mine. He returned after about ten minutes with two chicken sandwiches and another bottle of beer. There was only one bottle of beer this time and he didn't offer me another. He sat down and handed me a sandwich and we munched on in silence. My beer bottle was still more than half full and it was already going to my head. Tug finished his sandwich first then began to speak again.

"What aahh was just tellin' ye Jimmy med me think aboot lots of things. Aah've nivvor killed another thing since that day. No... I tell a lie cos I've put a few rabbits oot of their misery if aah've seen one with mixy ye knaa... wi' the bulging eyes and dyin' in agony. Aah've finished a few of them but it was to help them not hurt them. Me own hens live until they die natural... aah've nivvor killed another one of me own hens since 1946. What you're eatin' now came from me pal and aahh know it's still been killed but it wasn't me that did it so me conscience is clear. One of the other things me son said that day was 'dad there's only one thing wrong with this world we live in... and that's us, the humans. We're the only animal that kills for pleasure and not just for food. The day will come when we've killed all the animals on the planet and there'll be nowt left to murder other than each other'. He was right Jimmy... he was definitely right."

Now that Tug had unburdened with that little speech I thought it might be okay for me to speak. I left it for a little while then began.

"So what's the second one Tug? What's the other thing that changed yer life? It's alright if you don't want to say what happened."

Tug seemed relieved at the change in conversation and jumped right in.

"Ethel happened Jimmy… Ethel. One day aahh was just a young larrikin yem from sea and waitin' for me next ship. Me and Mordy had met up agen and we'd planned ter gan dancin' in Blyth at a church hall of all places. I'd put a clean collar on me shirt… cos collars were detachable then, cleaned my shoes and put my best strides on. Me jacket wasn't ower canny but aahh put some smelly stuff on it and gave it a good brush doon. Mind aahh had a pocketful of money so if aahh didn't get a lass ter dance with then aahh could always gan ter the pub. Anyways we gan into the dance and it's Mordy that spots her first."

"Seen thon lass ower there Tug? What a cracker she is man."

"Aahh wasn't lookin' ter be honest so aahh just says, gan on then Mordy ask her for a dance man."

"Divvent be daft man Tug she's way ower bonny for the likes of us. One of the hoi-polloi will be askin her up."

"Then aahh seen where he was pointin' man and she turned aroond and smiled and yer could have knocked me doon with a feather. Me legs were like jelly… me heart was hammerin' away fifty ter the dozen and aahh could hardly breathe. That lass just took me breath away… she was a right Bobby-dazzla. So aahh says ter Mordy… aall right then aah'll gan and ask her mesell. Mordy laughed at us man and he said aah'd nee chance." At that point Tug took a time out

145

then had another mouthful of beer and the remains of his sandwich before resuming the tale.

"That walk across the floor was the worst... and as it turned out... the best walk of my life. Aahh thought aahh was gannin ter flake oot man. Aahh was even practicin' what ter say when she knocked us back and gave us the bum's rush... that bit was funny an' all. So aahh gets there in front of her and she's waitin' for me ter speak and me voice is aall croaky... then aahh gan... 'errrmm, I errr was errrmm just err wonderin' like if errrmm yer might like ter have a dance with us like?"

"That would be very nice," she says.

"Well ye cannit blame a bloke for tryin'... aahh say as aahh turn to walk away cos that's the answer that aah'd rehearsed. Then it sinks in... she's just said yes. When aahh turn back she's laughing and that laugh was like music... nice music... classical stuff like a harp playin' and me... aahh just stand there grinnin' like a halfwit." Tug had a mile-wide smile across his face as the memory kicked in.

"As we start dancin me heart feels like it's gannin ter burst oot of me chest and she smells of lavender and aahh say... how come such a beautiful lass wants ter dance wi' me?"

She laughed at me and said, "You mean you don't know? It's because most beautiful lasses end up with plain looking men because the good-looking men like you are usually too scared to ask... so I'm glad you found the courage to do the walk of the brave."

"We call it the walk of shame, I say even though aahmm pleased as punch that she's called me good-looking."

"It's only called the walk of shame if you get a knock-back" she said "But I prefer to think of it as the 'sad walk' because there's a disappointed man who's just had a refusal. I'm glad we girls don't have to do it."

"With that she puts her head on me shoulder and her hair smells like a bowl of fruit... nice like, and aahhmm feelin' like a million dollars. So that's the other magic day that changed me life for ever Jimmy... the day aahh met me wife. That day aahh met the lass who took me breath away."

The beer has gone to my head by this time. A whole bottle of Double Maxim and I'm trying to pretend that I drink beer all the time and it doesn't affect me.

"So you're an old romantic Tug."

"Aahh wouldn't say that. There was only the one lass in me life after that. Aahh nivvor looked elsewhere ever agen. If yer lucky Jimmy it'll happen ter you one day. Someone will tek yer breath away."

"It's already happened man Tug. Ye don't need ter be owld to have them things happen ter ye."

"Aye Jimmy... as if. What's her name then... this lass who took yer breath away?"

I gave my head a big shake, "It wasn't a lass man Tug it was a lad."

Tug looked like he was right out of his comfort zone. He looked at me with a funny expression on his face. "A lad Jimmy... what yer on aboot? Some lad took yer breath away?"

"Aye Tug... it was Derek Raisbeck and he punched me in the stomach. Aahh couldn't breathe for ages." I began giggling like an idiot... the beer had worked its magic. Tug was laughing too but more out of relief than anything else.

I leaned back in my chair... then 'thummpp' I was flat on my back and had smacked my head on the path. I'd forgotten that I was sitting on the pouffe.

Tug helped me up. "Time we were getting inside Jimmy and sobering ye up or else yer dad will be ower ter give us hell." I didn't argue.

It was about an hour later that I left Tug's house that day. He'd sobered me up with some fizzy concoction and another chicken sandwich. Before I left he gave me a five-pound note and a packet of twenty tabs. That made me think something was going on that I didn't know about... but I didn't for a minute think that I'd never see him again and I didn't refuse the generosity.

It had been a good day.

Tug died the following week. I didn't find out until about a month later when I bumped into Mordy who was on a walk through the fields with Tug's dog Winston. I found that really weird in itself because Winston had been like Tug's shadow and never left his side. Strange then took on a new meaning because when we bumped into each other Winston trotted up to me and gave me a lick as if I was an old pal. It was the first time ever... and the last.

Tug had obviously known what was coming and had prepared all the groundwork. Winston now lived with Mordy and seemed pleased enough with the arrangement although Mordy told me that he was still very withdrawn. I was truly sad when I heard the news because I'd lost a friend and the world had lost an old codger the likes of whom we'll never likely see again.

I realised then that the fiver and the packet of tabs was Tug's farewell present to me and something I'll always remember. The tabs and the fiver didn't last long of course but the memory will.

Then my final two school years came and went but they didn't seem important anymore... and then real-life kicked in. But I always remembered the last talk Tug and I had about turning points in life and from that day on I began looking out for mine. It would be a lot of years before I finally had my moment but it would turn out to be like Tug had said. A happening that would turn my life on its head and change everything for the better.

To the best of my remembering this is how it happened.

CHAPTER 13

No Milk Today

———————————————◆———————————————

Hull 1983, it's April and still decidedly chilly... and with-it being Hull during a spell of low pressure the whole town stinks of fish. The smell permeates everything and clings to your clothes and over the past few years I've grown to hate it. High pressure, low pressure it didn't really matter... it was a truism during that particular period that you could smell Hull half an hour before you reached the town.

Unfortunately for me it's that time again when I'm stuck in the middle of one of my mentally down phases, having just cocked up my life big time yet again. I'd packed a brilliant job in at BP Chemicals, Saltend... top money and benefits, top bunch of pals and I'd just chucked it all up one day deciding I had bigger ambitions for my future and instead of producing chemicals I was going to sell them instead and make myself a fortune. It was more than a bad choice... it was disastrous.

I was four weeks into my new job as East Yorkshire area rep for Swan Chemicals an outfit based in Kendal and the first two weeks had gone down a storm. Orders every day from hospitals, from British Aerospace, Capper Pass, bus companies and half a dozen smaller orders from pubs. I was even mentioned in despatches in the Swan newsletter that made you feel good about yourself. My sales manager Dick Devlin had joined me for the Tuesday of my third week and we'd had a brilliant day together picking up three cracking orders with a really big one from Broadgate mental hospital which was somewhere out Beverley way. Surely it meant I was on my way to being a superstar. No unfortunately it didn't.

Because after that brilliant Tuesday... Wednesday happened. Not that Wednesdays were in any way to blame for my current plight. I was living on my own by this time in an upstairs flat in Glencoe Street having trashed yet another relationship... not sure how and not sure why but it was becoming a feature of my life... short term relationships quickly dissolved. That bleak Wednesday I didn't want to get out of bed. I didn't want to see anyone or go to work... or even go to the pub and that final piece of life's jigsaw made me realise there was something seriously wrong with the way I was existing... because I was usually an avid fan of the pub. I was at the bottom of a black hole. I wasn't sure how to climb out of it and just wanted to be left alone.

It was Friday, getting on for mid-morning before I surfaced. Three days in a row without making a single sales call and no human contact. There was no milk left in the fridge for my cornflakes... the bread in my breadbin and the chunk of cheddar in the fridge were both masquerading as petri dishes for penicillin – the bread stale and furry and the yellow cheddar now a weird blue colour in mouldy patches. Time indeed to rouse myself from this self-induced torpor.

I pulled on some jeans and a jumper and headed downstairs to see if there was any mail.

Indeed there was... at the front door there were two brown envelopes and a leaflet inviting me to give blood at my local clinic. I decided to give the blood donation invite a sidestep and headed back upstairs opening the envelopes as I climbed. One was a bill and I immediately gave it the contempt it deserved, giving it top spot on the growing pile of similar rubbish. The other envelope contained a cheque from Swan... my retainer and commissions from the previous week and it was quite a juicy amount. I was instantly cheered up. There was also a newsletter announcing myself as the shooting star for the week. I grimaced and wondered fleetingly what next week's newsletter would have to say about the current week's performance.

But who cared about next week? Now is what matters... the here and now because next week will look after itself I thought to myself. I'm back in funds and way more than I'd expected... I needed to get my skates on because the money wasn't going to spend itself... was it?

An hour later I'm skipping out of my Yorkshire bank branch with £200 in my pocket and there's another decent chunk of cash nestling in my account for rent and emergencies. First stop was the Master's Bar... and as it happened also the last stop of the afternoon. It was well after four when I eventually left after a sneaky afternoon lock-in. I departed with a belly-full of lager but my cash stash was still looking exceedingly healthy and a night on the town was in order... but therein lay the conundrum. I was too old to be hanging around Romeo's or Tiffany's – all the folk that frequented those night clubs looked to be about thirteen or fourteen and the Bali Hai nightclub was only decent on over 25s nights, known to us thirty-somethings as 'grab a granny' nights but unfortunately tonight wasn't it so I was at a bit of a loss.

So it was a Friday night sometime in late April 1983, date undecided... and there was myself 'Billy no mates' in my early thirties and heading for my local pub the Silver Cod on Anlaby Road. Usually I felt okay being on my own... in fact I usually preferred solitude but tonight I was feeling lonesome. For the first time in weeks I was needing some decent company but I wasn't going to get it at the Silver Cod.

That evening in particular I didn't know any of the male boozers and all the women were with partners, all but a few and those that weren't with partners were the kind of lasses you wouldn't have fancied three rounds in a boxing ring with. I didn't fancy perching on a bar stool that evening to make pointless conversation with a barmaid intent on just earning her evening wage so I sat alone in a corner.

Being alone in your own home is bearable, sometimes preferable, but being alone in a crowd is truly awful... you feel your loneliness acutely. That's precisely how I felt that night and my happy afternoon soon became painful.

I left after a few drinks... all taken in isolation then headed for the local off licence and chippy. A cheap bottle of whisky, a few packets of crisps and a haddock supper accompanied me on my lonely trek back to my flat. I'd forgotten to purchase milk – so black coffee it would be tomorrow morning... if there was any coffee left in the jar.

Then... the very next day came the turning point that Tug had told me would come along when least expected.

A blast from my past was about to turn my world upside down. A ghost was about to re-enter my life... and then argue, persuade, cajole and bully me into putting some substance into my very shallow and narcissistic lifestyle. I'd thought this person was dead and buried long ago, but no... I was mistaken. He wasn't... and his words and guidance would conjure up an immensely profitable period for myself which helped sort out my life and my future.

Black coffee with a few cold chips and batter left over from last night's supper was my breakfast feast that eventful Saturday... so a shopping trip was on the agenda. A quick shave and then a few bits of toilet roll stuck to my face to soak up the bloody nicks. I made a mental note to buy some razor blades for my shaver... and some cheap aftershave.

I hated shopping. It meant I was spending money on boring essentials when it could have been spent on fun and frivolity. I needed a new pair of jeans too and possibly a couple of shirts... and my work suit was needing a trip to the dry-cleaners, boring-boring-boring... and expensive.

I dodged the clothes buying for the time being and stocked up with some tinned goods, a box of eggs, a jar of jam, a few loaves of bread, a jar of coffee and a big pack of side bacon. That would see me through a good few days. New razor blades and the cheapest aftershave I could find finished off the shopping and I swiftly deposited my purchases in the flat... but what now?

Over the previous month or so I'd lost contact with all my old mates from BP... Martin Dixon, John Hart, Foppo Leuwerke and Ron Olsen. And as I'd quickly discovered a salesman works alone, and customers aren't friends... they're targets so once again I was on my own and at a loss. Football unfortunately was totally out of the question... this was a rugby league town with Hull and HKR being the big noises in the City and even at school I'd disliked rugby intensely. Football-wise there was only Hull City, and their ground - Boothferry Park was only a stone's throw away but they were in the third division and boring. Their stadium was like a council tip, falling to bits and rather than go watch them play I'd have preferred to poke myself in the eye with a sharp stick.

I decided to give the stick a miss and had a quick wash and fluff up of my hair. Then a splash of Hai Karate, a quick brush of the teeth, a squirt of the pits with Right Guard and a quick change into my going out clothes. And that was me primed for action. A drive out into the countryside for fresh fields and a mini adventure was on the agenda.

At the local garage I filled up the tank of my Nissan Bluebird then shook and straightened the back seat blanket just in case... and off I motored into the wild blue yonder. Well not quite the wild blue yonder... I thought I'd head out to Brantingham and see what the world had in store for me today. I'd heard there was a half-decent pub in the village and I'd never visited that particular hostelry... and who knew maybe I could even lay down a marker for future chemical sales. I'd had a good run the previous week selling channel blocks, degreaser and beer line cleaner to various pubs in and around Beverley area. I was beginning to feel a little more chipper... the head clouds were rapidly dispersing and I was entering an 'up' phase.

When I eventually found the Brantingham pub it was shut... for renovations or something so somewhat disappointed

I left the car in the pub car park and wondered over to the village green with its central duck pond. It was a lovely and peaceful little place and I lapped up the atmosphere. I sat myself down on the grass for a think and a cigarette. I was rolling my own by now, not for saving money I just preferred it and as I sat there constructing my smoke and watching the world go by a smartly dressed woman and roughly my age wandered over and stood beside me.

She stood quietly staring at the duckpond for a few seconds then, "You're not from around here," she began, "Are you lost or something... I saw you leaving your car at the pub," then she paused before continuing, "I'm not being nosey or anything... it's just that I know everyone in the village and for some reason you just looked a little lost."

I thought her comment over for a few seconds then responded, "How do you know I'm not from around here... Brough or Ferriby or somewhere?"

She laughed, "With a Geordie accent like that... I don't think so. The last time I heard something like your accent I was at my grandad's house in a place called 'Cambois'."

When she said it she made it sound like 'Camb-wahh' and it sounded silly like a French person saying it. A Blyth person would have pronounced it 'Cammiss' the way it was meant to be pronounced."

"You've been to Blyth then?"

"Yes... but I won't be going back. No offence but that part of the world just didn't sit right with me.

She was just being friendly, I relaxed and held up the baccy pouch and said, "Do you want a smoke." I smiled as I sparked my lighter up and lit my cigarette.

"I don't smoke... but thanks for asking. So are you just sightseeing?"

I decided to give my clever head a run-out, "Certainly not I'm a self-made millionaire... and I'm just deciding whether to buy the village or not." I grinned at her then, "Nah, I live in Hull, just off Anlaby Road. I've been down this area for about four years now but I can't seem to shake off the accent."

A little snort from her, "Don't bother trying it's much preferable to Hull speak... I aren't keen on it, can you borrow me a fiver, as the joskins and pattyslappers would say," she laughed as she parodied the local accent.

I didn't mind opening up to this lady for some reason so I continued. "I've never been out as far as this before. I just decided on a drive about and I'd heard from somewhere that the pub here was alright... but it's shut for renovations or something and I'm in desperate need of a pint."

She gave my reply some thought, then... "It's only my personal preference mind but if I were you I'd go back down the road and pop into the Green Dragon in Welton. The beer's good the folk are friendly and there's quite a bit of history attached to that particular pub."

The history comment made my ears prick up. Any sort of history, ancient or local was right up my street so I asked, "What sort of history?"

The reply was immediate, "You know... old stuff that happened in the past."

I had to give that comment a huge grin... she was toying with me, "Very funny ha-ha, seriously though I'm quite a fan of history... so what's the story with the Green Dragon?"

"Have you heard of Mrs Malaprop?" she asked.

The name rang a bell and I rummaged in my brain files for a few seconds, then I remembered... Mrs Malaprop was the character in a famous play who would use an incorrect word in place of a word with a similar sound resulting in a nonsensical sentence, "Aye, I have... we did 'The Rivals' at school... you know the Sheridan play... oh yes and wasn't Malaprop based on Dogberry in A Midsummer Night's Dream?"

"It must have been a good school," she commented and I think she was a little surprised at my Sheridan reply. "But I think you'll find Dogberry is in Shakespeare's 'Much Ado About Nothing.'" She corrected me. She was obviously well educated.

"It was good... my school I mean, Blyth Grammar School. Not that I was a great pupil... when it came to Shakespeare anyway."

She nodded an acknowledgement and began walking away. "The Green Dragon is reputedly where the final arrest of Dick Turnip took place."

I chuckled as she continued walking. She'd just hit me with a Malapropism. Then I shouted, "What's your name?" I wasn't being cheeky it was just that I'd noticed she wasn't wearing a wedding band.

She stopped and turned "Betty."

Now for a charm offensive, "I'm Jim... I don't suppose you fancy coming with me to that pub?"

She laughed, "You suppose correctly... sorry but no I can't."

I threw her a grin and gave a shrug then made the old 'Tug' withdrawal, "Can't blame a bloke for trying can you?

I'll saunter off alone to sort out Mr Turnip. It was nice talking with you have a good rest of the day."

She paused then... "I really am busy, I wasn't giving you the cold shoulder. I've seen you before now that I come to think of it. You might want to look in at the Bali Hai next week... over 25s night I'm sure I've seen you there." And with that she turned and walked away... then after a few paces half turned and smiled over her shoulder before carrying on.

That was the first surprise of the day and to be honest I didn't know if I'd just done a good or a bad thing. The second event was to be even more surprising and a complete gob-smacker.

CHAPTER 14

God Only Knows

———————————◼———————————

Have you ever experienced one of those days when the 'fate genie' jumps up and down in front of you grinning because he's just scrambled your brain with something completely unexpected? One of those days when out of the blue your journey through life takes a totally bizarre direction and it sends your whole perception of events into a tailspin? I have on several occasions since experienced those freaky turning points but that particular day was to turn out to be the Crown Jewels of thunderclap moments. My Tug life-change prophesy moment.

I found the Green Dragon without difficulty and it turned out to be homely and welcoming... although sparsely populated that afternoon. I ordered a pint of bitter and sat down at a table opposite the bar and proceeded to scan my newspaper. I was a Daily Mail reader at that time... way before it became a silly right-wing comic and being from the north-east I began to read it back to front from the sports pages. There were only four or five other folk dotted around the room and one young lass behind the bar. When I'd ordered my drink I'd asked her what she knew about this pub and Dick Turpin? and she'd just shrugged and said "I don't know... I not from here... there is information on posters, on wall." She'd sounded foreign so I decided not to go looking around the walls and took my seat. I wanted someone to tell me the history of the pub not look at pictures. Surely there'd be an informed local to ask shortly.

There wasn't much in my newspaper. Vauxhall had launched a new car called the Nova, the film Gandhi had won a load of academy awards... and we were to have a one-pound coin from Monday but the pound notes would remain legal tender for a few years... apparently. Sunderland looked safe in the First Division which was won by Liverpool again. That was about all the news apart from the political stuff and the Daily Mail Thatcher appreciation society so I rolled a cigarette and took out my pen for a crack at the crossword.

One across – a member of the tit family (5 letters). I was really frustrated to be stuck on the first clue. One down – Lord of all he surveys (6 letters). That one was easy – Kaiser but that created a problem... one across beginning with a K. A member of the tit family... it couldn't be Kite there weren't enough letters... it couldn't be Kestrel either... too many letters and anyway they were both birds of prey. I thought it could possibly be a political clue with it being the Mail but Kinnock wouldn't fit either. I wasn't having much success so I turned my attention to the white-haired old bloke who'd wandered in a few minutes ago. I hadn't given him much of a glance when he entered because I was busy messing up my crossword but maybe he'd be my local historian.

The man was sitting at the bar with his back to me chatting with the barmaid... and they were chatting in a foreign language. I wasn't familiar with any of the words I overheard but I did know it wasn't French or German because I had a smattering of both from my schooldays. I didn't think it could be Italian either because I hadn't overheard 'mama mia' or 'ciao bella' or seen any flapping hands. My language knowledge was somewhat limited but with what little knowledge I did possess I reckoned it must be one of the east European dialects they were speaking.

The man stopped chatting to take a swig from his pint and half turned. He had a thick white beard and moustache to match his hair... think Santa Claus and you'd be close to what I was seeing. He wasn't smartly dressed... but he wasn't shabby either. A pair of black trousers, black boots and a combat jacket. The combat jacket rang a few memory bells in my head... but surely not. He turned back to the barmaid and began talking again. I noticed her leaning closer to the man and pointing towards myself whilst talking in not much more than a whisper.

The old guy turned slowly to face me and in that moment frozen in time I was stunned... hit broadside on with a bolt from the blue.

The old man's face and head looked as if they were covered in thick white fluffy cotton wool... but the eyes... the eyes were blue and piercing and those same eyes had pierced my own many-many moons ago, at least twenty years at quick calculation... maybe more. Everything else about the man had aged considerably but those eyes could only belong to one person... it was Charlie Chuck. He's been Sid Brown's old mentor from our schooldays and the man who'd saved my bacon on a few occasions and he was staring hard in my direction. It took a moment or two but then the fluff around his mouth parted as he gave a huge smile.

I was transfixed... open mouthed. I couldn't get my head around seeing this apparition from my past. I could only watch silently as he eased himself from his bar-stool... making an old man grunting noise as he stood up slowly and gingerly before moving over to my table and putting down his drink on a spare beer mat before sitting down.

Silence reigned for a good few seconds before it was broken by Charlie. A big fluffy smile then "Hello James... it is you isn't it?"

I couldn't reply. My word box was completely empty. I just stared at him and tried to crack a smile but my attempt must have appeared more like an awkward smirk... this couldn't be happening.

"Cat got your tongue?"

I wished I could have taken my response and stuffed it back into my mouth but I couldn't. "Charlie man... it can't be you. What are you playing at? you're supposed to be dead."

Charlie gave a wry smile. "Thought I'd give it a miss... it's an overrated state of affairs."

My sensible head still wasn't functioning properly, "Sorry Charlie... I didn't mean that I wished you were dead. It's just that I assumed you were too old to still be alive."

Charlie Chuck chuckled. "You're still a master of the graceless comment James... but remember that Methuselah was nine-hundred or more when he died so I still have a way to go yet. By the way I'm only eighty-six so I'm nowt but a toddler in biblical terms."

"Sorry Charlie, that was ignorant."

"Don't be sorry Jim because I'm as shocked to see you as you are to see me. What on earth are you doing sitting in a pub in a village like Welton?" before I could answer he noticed my unfinished crossword and pulled my newspaper across the table, scanned my pathetic attempt and after a few silent moments of studying he said. "I think you'll find that one down is master not Kaiser, and one across is Marsh... one of the six or seven species of tit here in the UK.

"Yeh I knew that."

"Of course you did Jim," he said, giving me a doubtful look, then "So what are you doing here... on holiday perhaps?"

"No Charlie I live in Hull now. I've been here in various jobs for the past four years. I've got a flat in Glencoe Street just off Anlaby Road."

"Aye I know Glencoe Street. Is it your flat?"

"Only until I stop paying the rent." Charlie had begun his digging and I'd heard this line of questioning many years ago. I didn't want him digging any deeper. "It suits my purposes for now Charlie it's just temporary... until I make a few decisions. Anyway enough about me. What are you doing here in Welton... hiding yourself away?"

He smiled when replying, "No James certainly not, I'm just having a lazy day out. I've been visiting friends as it happens. So to repeat what are you doing here in Welton?"

I knew from old that Charlie would just keep on asking until he got a straight answer... he hadn't changed one iota. So I answered, "I've just come out to meet a lass in

Brantingham." That explanation was a little disingenuous but at least it was on the almost true side.

"So you're either not married or you're playing away." Charlie's knack for drawing you in obviously hadn't abated over the years. The statement couldn't be ignored.

"I'm not married... not now Charlie and it's pointless asking about the lass because I've only just met her. All I know is that she's a good looker, she's intelligent and she's into Mrs Malaprop. She couldn't come with me today but she directed me down here to the Dick Turnip pub."

"Ha-ha I like it... the Malapropism very droll. I'll have to repeat that one at my next Alcoholics Unanimous meeting."

"Do you go to?" ... then I stopped myself as Charlie's response malapropism filtered through to my brain... 'alcoholics unanimous' indeed.

Charlie seemed pleased that I'd understood his play on words and he continued, "So, where do you work... or do you work?" Charlie ploughed on in the same vein unabated. But enough was enough, all this 'anything you do say may be used in evidence' questioning was making me feel uncomfortable. That bit of Charlie had stood the test of time... he asked direct questions and he expected direct answers.

"Charlie... come on man enough about me. I've a few things to sort out to get my life back on track... end of story I'm not a kid anymore. I want to know your story. Why did you go missing from everyone's life and what have you been doing in the meantime?"

Charlie gave a nod acknowledging the question then pointed to my baccy pouch which was lying open on the table. "Can you knock one of those up for me Jim... not a skinny one? I can't do it very well nowadays what with the arthritis in the hands... and the shakes. I'll get Magda to bring us some drinks over. What's your poison? Just bitter?"

"Aye please," I replied as I took his request on board and began working at knocking up two rollies, "A single malt chaser wouldn't go amiss either Charlie but I'll buy that myself." I wasn't used to rolling fat cigarettes... mine were usually extremely thin fellows which in my thinking made the pouch last longer. I succeeded nevertheless.

Charlie gestured to the barmaid and gave his order in what I reckoned was Polish with a flourish of hand signals as if he were doing that deaf signing thing. A few minutes later the barmaid who I now knew as Magda placed a tray on our table. There were two pints of bitter, two large whiskies and two fat pasties which for some reason were sitting on a bed of lettuce and accompanied by a little dish of brown sauce and a plastic spoon. Two paper plates and two paper napkins completed the line-up. I thought to myself that I needed to learn those hand signals... they certainly got the business done.

Cigarettes now constructed I passed the fattest of the two to Charlie and he reached for my lighter and sparked up. "Thank you Jim," he said as he drew in a lungful and exhaled a grey cloud, "God is good sometimes," he muttered with eyes closed and a euphoric look on his hair festooned features. "My first puff for almost a month."

I was a little worried that he might set his beard on fire but I had to grin as I watched my blast from the past in his state of rapture. "Have you been trying to pack the smoking in Charlie? I feel awful," I said guiltily.

Charlie gave a contented smile and his eyes opened slowly, "Not really Jim just chewing lots of Wrigley's gum and I've been avoiding those who would lead me astray... and God in his infinite wisdom led me to you so it must be his fault, part of his plan... there's no need for you to feel awful it was me who asked you for a roll-up... not the other way around."

"These pasties look nice Charlie," I said changing the subject with conscience now assuaged after Charlie's last comment, "but she hasn't brought any forks I'll just go and ask."

"No fork required Jim eat them the Ukrainian way... and as the big fella up in the sky intended. Just break them open and use your fingers."

"Ehhh... really?"

"Of course really. Where in the bible does it say 'And God looked down on the garden of Eden and seeing his plight gave unto Adam a fork to eat his pastie? It didn't happen."

We both stubbed out our cigarettes and attacked the pasties. Charlie looked like Santa Claus feasting on mince pies. I was having difficulty laughing with a mouthful of pastry and only just managed to stop myself from covering Charlie in squelch. As instructed I tucked in bare-handed, spooning in the brown spicy sauce and I thoroughly enjoyed the mini feast washed down with a pleasant pint of bitter. I couldn't help but smile though because Charlie hadn't been lying about the shaky hands and he had more pastie in his beard than had made it to his mouth. But he looked content, a man at peace with his life. I was desperate to learn his secret.

As much as I'd been wanting Charlie's secret of life... it turned out that there was no secret to be told... no great revelation. Charlie was just living his life one day at a time and making the very best of each day as it came. I can honestly recall that time like it was yesterday and that was the occasion when I just sat back... listened and learned. I didn't know it at that moment but I would be soaking up information and guidance like a sponge over the following few months... with Charlie as my mentor.

It was fascinating to hear this man tell his story and lay it all out without a hint of fabrication or falsehood. I firmly believe that Charlie Chuck had been sent into my life at that juncture by a higher force, I honestly do... because the effect it was to have on my life was profound.

Charlie must have talked for best part of an hour laying out the time-line of the previous twenty or so years. At times the chronology just wouldn't fit but I didn't care... it was fascinating so I sat still and listened. This man was on a different plane to myself... he had a view of life that I could only struggle to understand but sometimes the struggle begets the understanding of perfection. I realised early on that as far as perfection was concerned for myself that ship had sailed but I could still aim higher than the low point my life was currently mired in. Perhaps one day I'd attain mediocrity... and I said as much.

Charlie disagreed.

"Mediocrity is where we all begin our lives James unless you're one of the entitled rich. Mediocre is your median point and it's up to you whether you fly above the line or sink below it. In all our meetings when I knew you in Blyth you never struck me as the kind of lad who would end up sinking."

That comment gave me pause for thought but I didn't reply because Charlie didn't dwell on it. The drinks kept coming as he laid out a description of his life since leaving Blyth... and in the main it was absorbing stuff.

Then it was my turn to lay out the timeline of my life. Because the drinks had been flowing my guarded hesitancy disappeared and I opened up in a way that I hadn't managed for many years. Somehow Charlie just sucked you in and squeezed out the truth... he was just a bloke with a knack of making interrogation seem like normal conversation.

He seemed quite concerned when I told him how my life was just an unending sequence of huge highs and depressing lows with seemingly no middle ground. I talked for ages... and everything came tumbling out... the good, the bad and the ugly but it didn't make me feel wretched or shabby... in fact it seemed like a huge weight was lifting from my shoulders. I talked and talked until I'd covered every last blade of grass in describing the wilderness that had been the battlefield for my erratic lifestyle.

We left the Green Dragon together both rather sozzled and Charlie insisted on taking my car keys from me and parking the car up at the pub until the following day and until I'd sobered up. We took a taxi together and I ended up spending the night on Charlie's couch in his Pearson Park flat.

The following day after we'd picked up my car Charlie began to assume his mentoring mantle and went to work on me and my lifestyle as only Charlie could. He began taking my life apart and then putting the pieces back together like a jigsaw. The man was like an alpine avalanche... an unstoppable force and if you were in its path it just swept you away. Why Charlie felt the need to take me under his wing I'll never know but I'll always be grateful for the time he invested in me.

Five weeks later I was sitting in a doctor's office in Chanterlands Avenue waiting for a prognosis from a consultant in private practice whom I'd been seeing at Charlie's insistence. Charlie had the knack of taking over your life and shoehorning it into places you didn't know existed. During those weeks I'd seen three different specialists and undergone two medical trials and a barrage of psychological tests. On top of that I was no longer working as a chemical sales rep but instead I was signing on... a gentleman of leisure and spending all my spare time in the library. Today however I was to hear the informed opinion of the collective mighty minds who'd had me under observation. Initially I'd thought the whole process to be some foolish charade because in my mind there was nothing wrong with me but the psychology guy had unnerved me somewhat with questions which didn't make sense.

Q "Who do you believe to be more important... the Queen or your mother?"

"My mother."

"Why?"

"Cos the Queen's never made my breakfast."

Q "Which day do you think is more important... the day you're born or the day you die?"

"Neither."

"Why?"

"Because you can't remember either of them."

Q "If you and your father were the same age do you think you'd be pals?"

"No."

"Why not?"

"If we were the same age he couldn't be my father."

Q "Who have been the three most important people in your life?"

"Charlie Chuck, Tug and Sid."

"Why?"

"Dunno, they just came into my head."

Q "If you wanted to kill someone what would be your chosen method... gun, knife or bomb?"

I thought about my answer for a while... much longer than the allotted five seconds. "Knife," was my reply even though I'd been timed out.

"Why?"

"A knife is easier to get hold of and more personal because you have to get up close. I wouldn't know where to get a gun but even so I might miss and hit someone else. A bomb could kill lots of innocent people and you still wouldn't know if you'd been successful because there'd be arms and legs and bits of folk all over the place." That answer had him scribbling furiously.

Q "What is your relationship with God?"

"I like him... he gave me a lift once."

"What?"

"He gave me a lift once... Charlie Hurley."

He looked puzzled, "You think this Charlie Hurley fellow is God?"

"Yes... he's the only one I've ever seen... well him and Eric Clapton." That had him scribbling too.

On that first occasion he spent an hour firing questions that I just couldn't see the point of but nonetheless I answered to the best of my ability and didn't have my clever head on. I was waiting for the 'why do you think all sheep in Wales have a nervous disposition'... but that one never surfaced. Subsequent visits to the psychologist however produced more nuanced questions and I began to relax into the routine.

Today however I was expecting the verdict and I really did feel like a prisoner in the dock waiting for the jury to return.

I needn't have worried because that day Mr Fischer the head consultant was very succinct. Giving me a smile as he entered the room he sat down and didn't mess around. Referring to a folder which he'd placed on the desk in front of him he came straight to the point and to the diagnosis. Polite he certainly was but the bloke was away with the fairies if he thought I understood any of his long and complicated neurological terms.

For the next five minutes he bombarded me with information about my brain. Neurotransmitters – serotonin – norepinephrine – hippocampus - frontal-lobe - limbic-cortex. Imagine Einstein attempting to explain relativity theory to a Greggs sausage roll and you'll have an idea of our relationship during those five long minutes. Everything went way over my head. Inside I was shouting 'will you get on with it man and stop parading your intellect you pompous prat'. In reality though I was giving the occasional smile and pretending to be totally absorbed in his presentation. He seemed happy anyway.

"So James as you'll have gathered from what I've been saying you have a chemical imbalance in the brain."

"Okay... nae bother."

"And this causes your extreme highs and your depressing lows."

"Righto... got it. So what's the answer... how do I deal with it?"

Mr Fischer produce a bottle of pills from his pocket. "With these James. I've contacted your GP with my diagnosis and recommendations. He concurs so he'll continue with future prescriptions. You'll have to make an appointment to see him as soon as possible because I've only given enough tablets for fourteen days and your GP will need to monitor the result."

"So, will these things sort me out... you know, get me back on track?" I reached for the bottle and scanned the label.

"To a certain extent yes. But it will require input from yourself. These pills aren't magic but they'll help to even out the ups and downs. Your journey through bi-polarity didn't make you manic on the ups or suicidal on the downs. Fortunately your journey was milder... less severe, so the outcome should be pretty much successful. Your doctor may refer to the diagnosis as clinical depression and that's acceptable. He may also need to amend the dosage or prescribe an alternative depending on your reaction to the medication."

"So I won't be nutty anymore?"

Mr Fischer smiled. "You were never nutty James. A chemical imbalance is just another ailment. If you had a broken leg or were suffering from influenza then everyone would be able to see the problem while your ailment has for the main part been hidden in plain sight. Now we begin the journey to smooth out the bumps and confront the demons from your past."

"Ehhh?"

"Your input James."

"I don't understand."

"The tablets will smooth out the mood swings but you need to confront those times when you felt unable to cope with life. When you were either up and ready to set the world alight or conversely you were down and wanting to hide away. Revisit those times James... the ones you can remember and see them for what they were... just life throwing up its vagaries. Face them then ditch them. There's no need to be locking those moments away inside your head any longer. Bring them out into the light of day and give them an airing... because believe me you will feel eminently more comfortable with your new state when you've shaken out those cobwebs."

With that final speech he stood up, closed and picked up his folder then nodded in my direction. "Good luck with your new life James... it's been a pleasure." Then he turned and left without another word.

I was pleased with the outcome and so was Charlie. The very next week after the tablets had a chance to work their magic I began talking about those times that Fischer had wanted airing. I was lucky to have such a sympathetic mentor as Charlie paying attention to my unburdening. I began to talk and Charlie listened and it was cathartic. Charlie told me to deal with the oldest memories first. So I did and he sat and listened as I began my journey with the memory of a man called Gilbert. "Come on then James... fire away."

CHAPTER 15

School's Out For Ever

———————————————————•———————————————————

Remembering that first bunch of highs and lows was easier than I'd imagined. Now that I'd been given licence to unshackle by brainbox it came as an unexpected release when I faced those skeletons. Furthermore... when I'd pulled them out of their cupboard I realized that they could never go back inside.

The first memory that surfaced was of a day when Titch hadn't managed to persuade his mam to let him accompany me to the pictures. He was in his mam's bad books for some naughty behaviour and wasn't allowed privileges such as a trip to the afternoon movies. I was disappointed but as I hadn't anyone else to go with I decided not to back out completely and I went alone. Today's offering was a cowboy movie, maybe the 'Range Rider' or the 'Cisco Kid' with a load of cartoons as the 'B' offering.

The 'Essoldo' was sparsely populated that particular afternoon and I sat alone half way down the rows of seats somewhere in the middle. I was seven years old and very independent. The cowboy movie had me on the edge of my seat and I was enjoying every minute. Those cowboy movies were brilliant because loads of baddies were shot but none of them ever bled and all the horses that fell down always got up again and ran away. It may have been the 'Range Rider' but it didn't matter because you knew who to cheer for because the goodies had white hats and the baddies had black hats. It was like a western uniform.

The Indians on display always slapped their hands to their mouths and made attacking sounds like 'Yip yee – yip-yip yee' and they always went to the top of the nearest hill and made a smoky fire that they put their blanket over to make smoke signals like a nineteenth century e-mail. That was so they could communicate with their other tribe members who were miles away feasting on jerky and dancing around the Totem pole. Everybody knew that was the way the west worked and we kids were experts. Even so it always confused me when one of the goodies... who was being chased by the tribe would turn around in his saddle as his horse galloped along and fire one shot. How come that one shot always made six redskins fall off their horses? It was a mystery.

"Want a sweetie son?" A packet appeared in front of me at the end of an arm which belonged to a man sitting in the row behind.

It was a stupid question really because you'll never find a seven-year-old lad who doesn't want a free sweet. Anyway they were some sort of jelly sweet and I loved those ones. I took one from the packet.

"Ta mister."

The next thing I know he's sitting beside me. He was an ugly bloke wearing a long brown raincoat type thing. He didn't smell very nice either and had missing teeth.

I immediately felt uncomfortable. "Get some more sweets," he said as he flourished the paper bag in front of me.

I took a sweet out of the packet and at the same time I felt his free hand going underneath my short trousers heading for my willy. I was only seven but I knew this wasn't right.

"Aahmm tellin the woman on ye," I jumped up and moved quickly away from this predator. He tried to pull me back but I squirmed away... knocking the sweet packet from his hand as I did so and the sweets were scattering all over the floor. I ran as quickly as possible in the confined space between the rows of seats... and I was scared.

I ran to the woman at the back of the auditorium. She was flashing her torch at me as I ran up the aisle.

"And where are you off to in such a hurry young man?"

"That dirty man down there he's been rude. He's doing rude things."

The lady flashed her torch in the direction I pointed. He'd moved. Now he was sitting all innocent on the end seat of another row. "That's him missus the scruffy man."

The woman gave a rueful smile. "That's Gilbert son... I'll have a word with him. He's not all there," she said as she tapped a finger to her temple.

"Are you getting the police?"

"No... the police will just tell him off... so I'll do it instead." She made as if to walk away but I wasn't happy.

"Are you going to kick him out then?"

"No, it wouldn't do any good because he'll just come back. Go and sit somewhere else and I'll keep an eye on him."

Inside me I knew this wasn't right but I didn't know how to deal with the situation. I did have the courage to speak up though. "I'm gonna tell me mam and she'll come and tell him off. She might tell you off an' all for not doing anything. And she'll tell the police." With that I left the Essoldo and made a beeline for home. I'd only seen half a film and I was annoyed.

I must have ran all the way to Axwell Drive, "You're home sharp... has the projector broke down or something?" My mam was rolling out pastry on the kitchen table as I came in through the back door. Her pinny was covered in flour. For some reason she didn't have a proper rolling pin and she was using an empty milk bottle.

I had lots to say and it all came out in a rush, "Titch couldn't go with me. His mam wouldn't let him cos he was being told off for something so I went myself and a nasty man put his hand up my pants in the pictures."

Mam didn't answer. She was concentrating on fitting pastry to a big plate and trimming the edges off with her little sharp knife. I sat myself down at the kitchen table and watched her as she began flattening another pastry batch with her milk bottle roller. She seemed to be ignoring my revelation.

"Aahh just said that a rude dirty man called Gilbert put his hand up my pants."

"I'll see to it Jim... I'll see to it. Now will you just shut up and stop going on about it. And don't ever go to the pictures on your own again." She held her hand up in the air and with my mam that gesture signified the discussion was over and she'd had the last word. Don't go to the pictures on your own again was her solution. I didn't like it then but I understand it now. My mother didn't know what to do. I'd dropped a problem on her doormat and she was struggling. We kids expect our parents to know everything... to have all the answers but they don't. My mam genuinely didn't know what to do so she blagged it with a 'don't go to flicks alone' answer.

That was my first sortie against the demons in my head and Charlie and I were both pleased that this one had been cast out.

"What has that taught you James about hidden memories?... perhaps that confrontation trumps obfuscation?"

"I don't know where that one came from Charlie. I hadn't thought about that day for years... maybe for ever. It just came out without me having to think about it."

"Good but what have you learned from that?"

I knew precisely what I'd learned from it. "That it wasn't my fault Charlie and it wasn't my mother's fault either. She wasn't to blame and I've probably had her marked down as guilty all these years. She was confronted with a situation she didn't know how to handle. If it was anyone's fault then it was the perpetrator... a sad person with mental issues."

Charlie nodded and smiled, "Maybe you'll forgive your mother now James because you've never been close have you?"

I had to think about that for a while. "I understand the blame thing Charlie... and that occasion wasn't anyone's fault but there was more going on than that in those years."

"Okay... so spill the beans... get it out of your head and into your mouth," Charlie knew how to draw you out. So I began.

29 Axwell was in uproar. I'm eight years old and watching our new telly... our first telly. There would be no more

going next door to the Nichol house to watch the childrens' programmes. We've had the set for a few weeks now but it is still hypnotic. I can't keep my eyes off it no matter what is on because it's like being at the mini cinema. It's early evening and I'm sitting on the couch facing the telly and watching the box but behind me there is shouting and screaming and slapping sounds. My dad... who is one of Blyth's most mild-mannered men is giving my sister a right leathering. He's slapping her daft and my mam is stood with her back against the wall and she's just watching. She should be stopping the carnage because men don't hit women and my sister is sixteen now so that makes her nearly a woman. She isn't at school anymore and she even goes to work at Bolckows' the ship breakers at north Blyth and has to use the chain ferry to get there. That's impressive.

My sister is screaming and crying and dad is getting stuck in as if it was a boxing match and I can't ignore it anymore. It's inside my head now and I know what's going on isn't right. If no-one else is going to help wor Ann then it will have to be me. I jump up and run around the couch. Dad is just about to deliver another slap but I fling myself at him shouting, "Leave her alone you fat pig." Dad pushes me away with such force that I stagger backwards and hit my head on the sitting room door. That's not going to stop me though because I'm enraged with the unfairness of it all and I go back in for seconds. Mam is still just standing there... blank and watching and I jump in and start flailing away and hitting my dad because my sister is on the floor by this time and she's crying her eyes out.

Then dad stops. He's parrying the kid punches I'm throwing at him and he wraps his arms around me to pin my arms to my side... then he begins to cry. I've never seen my dad cry... it comes as a shock. After a few seconds he sets me free from the arm vice and he walks out of the room without another word. A few minutes later we hear the front door slam and through the front window we see dad pushing arms into jacket and stomping off down the street towards the Red House. Dad isn't a drinker so that is a surprise. Everything goes quiet in the house with just the occasional sniffle from my sister. Mam hasn't said a word during the entire happening.

It's 11.00 pm and mam has made me stay up for company. "Mam aahh want to go to bed."

"Ye'll go when aahh say... and not before." That was me told.

My sister is hiding away upstairs in her bedroom. Mam has been drinking sherry and it's the first time I've ever seen her have alcohol. She's tipsy. Dad hasn't returned as yet and that's strange. Mam isn't in the best of moods and I've never seen her this upset before.

Then there's a knock at the front door. Mam totters off to answer it. I can hear a woman's voice at the door and a thump as my dad comes in the house and falls over. Then there's laughing... two women laughing and I know the other woman's voice... it's Mrs Armstrong from along the street. I don't know why mam's laughing because everyone is frightened of Mrs Armstrong... mam included. Then dad comes into the sitting room. He gestures at me to vacate the couch which I do and he collapses onto it face down. 'Jings help ma boab' as 'Oor Wullie' would have said because my dad couldn't half snore. In fact I imagine that somewhere in

Blyth records he's probably listed as having been the Cowpen and Crofton snoring champion. After a few minutes I hear Mrs Armstrong leave and happily there's no more ructions that evening and everything goes back to normal.

It turned out that my sister had broken the news that evening that she was pregnant and my dad had flipped his lid. Okay that didn't warrant the kicking off and the leathering but at least it explained the situation and made the reaction understandable even though extreme. Then to cap it all dad had gone to drown his sorrows at the Red House and three pints later had set all the Axwell tongues a wagging because in his intoxicated state he'd walked into the wrong house and took himself off to bed in the Armstrong house... 25 Axwell. Mrs Armstrong was fearsome but even so she laughed herself silly at dad's antics because he'd walked in through the front door and headed upstairs straight for the bedroom. He started shouting when he got upstairs, "Whee's pinched the carpets Peg? Some bugger's gone and nicked wor carpets man." Mrs Armstrong didn't take offence with the no carpets comment and she brought Dad home with some difficulty it has to be said and his silly behaviour was the talk of the street for a few days.

I waited when I'd finished my story for some reaction but Charlie didn't comment on that one. I think he realised that I was quite capable now of working through my own head and making sense of those happenings that were coming to the surface. He took a back seat from that moment on and just listened. I was grateful for that.

It's June 1966 and everyone is looking forward to the World Cup which would be kicking off in just a few short weeks. At school there'd been a lot of illness amongst the teaching staff and we never knew who would be standing at the front of the class for our lessons. Eltringham, Rowland, Foggo, Green, Hunter and Sprawling have been missing for more than a week. The exams were over now and there was the cushy feeling of everything winding down as we approached July and the summer holidays. It's our English Literature lesson and we have a gawky young bloke at the front of the class... our supply teacher. He took us earlier in the week and we'd been tasked with writing a lyric poem in the style of Wordsworth's Daffodils. I'd actually made a good fist of it and had been pleased with my effort but I was well aware that with Dennis Tait and Alan Potter in the class there were likely to be some comedic submissions. The poor bloke really didn't have a chance with our 4-West reprobates because learning was now on the back burner and fun was the order of the day. He seemed to take an intolerably long time to sort out the pile of submissions before putting the bulk of them on his desk and standing at the front of the class with just one sheet in his hand.

"A good effort from some of you and not so good from others. But whoever wrote this particular piece of rubbish is an idiot," he said as he waved a sheet of paper around. "Signed Edgar Allan Potty and a really sad and pathetic attempt at humour. So which of you is the imbecile? Would the class idiot please stand up." He was being very forceful for a stand-in teacher.

There was no movement from any of the pupils.

"No... no-one got the courage? Didn't think so. It would take guts for an idiot to stand up."

Another few seconds passed before the scraping of a chair could be heard. All heads turned as Denis Tait stood up and faced the teacher.

"Well-well-well, surprise upon surprise. I don't know your name."

"Tait sir."

"Tait... So you're the class idiot?"

Tait smiled, "Actually I'm not sir. I just didn't want to see you standing up there on your own."

A gale of laughter swept the room and one thoroughly rattled teacher admitted defeat. To be honest it had never been a fair contest from the outset. And so it ended... 4-West (1) – Teacher (0).

Even Charlie laughed at that one. After a while we settled into a comfortable kind of question-and-answer session. Then Charlie dropped his bombshell. He fixed me with his eyes and then smiled before beginning.

"It's time for you to leave the nest James."

"Ehhh... what ye on about?" Charlie wasn't making sense.

"You've been a late flier James but the late fliers always seem to soar the highest. It's time for you to go."

I hadn't a clue what he was on about or leading to. "I think you'll find I'll be around for a while yet Charlie."

"No you won't James. It's time for you to leap into the future that's beckoning now that you've got your Charlie... and Tug in a bottle." He was referring to my supply of tablets which evened out my serotonin levels. "And you certainly need to curtail your pretend life and live the real one."

"Ehhh?"

"You know... like the pretend degree that got you the Stylo job and then the BP job?"

"Aye but Charlie I needed the jobs and anyway it worked."

"I realise that James but you know how I feel about the truth and there was no substance to your actions... just pretence. And believe it or not... sticking a python down your pants doesn't make you Errol Flynn."

That made me laugh but I still didn't understand the 'leaving the nest' comment. "Charlie man you're talking daft. Anyway just cos I've got my head sorted doesn't mean that I'm going to stop coming around to see you or going out for a pint with you."

Charlie opened up a baccy tin and took out a roll-up. I'd made twenty for him because Charlie couldn't roll them himself even with the little machine. Charlie was now back to smoking regularly but I'd given up feeling guilty. He didn't offer me one so I reached over and took one from his tin anyway. We both lit up before he continued the conversation.

"It's time for you to go and shine James. You've got about fifty years in front of you to right the mistakes of your first thirty. Go and set the world on fire James because I won't be around to see the flames."

I knew that Charlie was a linguist but just at that moment it seemed he was talking double Dutch. What on earth did he mean about not being around. He seemed in canny health so surely he couldn't be dying. I asked anyway.

"Are ye dyin' or something Charlie?"

Charlie laughed, "We're all dying James from the day we're born. The only certainties in our existence... apart from taxes are birth and death. We can't escape either of them but what defines our lives are the ways in which we fill in the gap between those two constants."

Charlie was being very philosophical although I couldn't let go without a fight. This bloke had just given me my Tug life-change moment. I wanted to hang on to that for as long as possible.

"So you're not dyin' Charlie... or I mean you are dyin' but not about to do it imminently? Aahh bugger... I don't know what I mean."

Charlie nearly choked on a mouthful of smoke as he laughed and gasped both at the same time. "Calm yourself down James... I'm not leaving this life just yet but I am leaving England."

"Ehhh?"

"I'm going to Sweden James."

"Aahh right you're off on holiday."

Charlie shook his head as he ground out his cigarette in the ashtray. "No James... I'm off to start the next part of my life. I'm off to an island in the Baltic called Gotland and I'm going to live and die there."

"What?"

"Family James... family. I have a nephew with a wife and family. I didn't know anyone had escaped the Russian onslaught... at least any family members. We were all marked down for termination you see. We were a family of academics and Russia can't tolerate people who can think for themselves.

"Russia Charlie? I thought you fought the Germans."

"The Germans were evil and ruthless but nowhere near as depraved as the Russians. I am Ukrainian not Russian.

My land was a civilized nation when St Petersburg was still a collection of mud huts. I fought against both of those evil empires until I couldn't do it anymore and had to leave with Martha before they tracked us down."

"So?"

"So I leave next week for a town called Visby. I was contacted by an old chum from British Intelligence and he gave me the news of my one remaining family member who had made it into Sweden. He was just a young lad at the time and lost all his family too. He had no idea that myself and Martha had made good our escape. Jerzy is so excited to be able to see me again... his own bloodline."

"But Charlie..."

"Don't be disappointed for yourself James be happy for your old friend Charlie who is off on a big adventure to spend his twilight years with his relatives. I don't know how many years I have left. Very few certainly. But my life is just about to complete its circle James...and that's something I thought would never happen. Be happy for me."

To be honest I was gobsmacked but Charlie was waiting expectantly for some positive response. "Of course I'm happy for you Charlie... really happy. It's just a bit of a shock to know I won't see you again and after all you've done for me and my mixed-up head."

"Ha-ha-ha your head is now unmixed James," Charlie chuckled, "But for heaven's sake it's only Sweden not Australia. You can come and visit and chew over old times just as soon as I get settled. I'm sure my nephew and his family would like to meet you too. It would make my life in England seem more real to them you know."

"Okay... fair do's Charlie I'll look forward to it."

"Yes but don't leave it too late... if you know what I mean."

"I'll be over there pot-hot just as soon as I sort Hull out."

"Don't spend much more of your life here in Hull James. You need to head back to your homeland and come to terms with your past. Make your peace with your birthplace and the town of your growing up years. I know you're conflicted about your Blyth years but Blyth has never been the culprit only the location. It may be a good idea to search out those folk you lived your formative years with. Sidney perhaps and Millie. Your old pal Titch. You've family in Blyth James, a mam and dad... a sister and a nephew. Cousins and aunties, old pals and old sparring partners. Memories James... memories. Go and relive them... then box them up. Give the bad memories a punch in the belly and tell them not to come back then tell the good ones how welcome they are and take them with you into your future."

I had to laugh at Charlie in full flow. He was an awesome sight and must have been a formidable teacher in his younger years. "Don't you ever give up with the control-freak attitude Charlie?"

"I don't know what you mean," he snorted "I call it being helpful. I look on this latest interlude with you as my swan song."

"Swan song... what are ye on about?"

"Swans reputedly sing a beautiful song just before they die. It's their parting gift to the world before they leave this life to meet up with their ancestors and their missing family. I'm using a metaphor James. My swan-song has been helping put your life back together... and believe me it's more preferable

189

than hearing me burst into proper song. I don't intend to meet my maker just yet but it's my final act in this country. I hope you'll make the most of it."

"Aye I suppose... of course I will, but when do you leave Charlie?"

He paused before replying, "I definitely don't want any silly send-off shenanigans mind you. No offence intended and I know your life has changed somewhat with your new medication but I don't want any daft balloons and strippers and stuff. I'm too old for that carry-on James."

"Aahh would never think of it Charlie," I winked, "I'd like to say ta'ra though if that's okay."

"Hmmm, I've a lot to do to get my documentation together and the correct visa information. It's quite complicated because I'm applying for permanent residency although I do have some official help from old comrades. Anyway if you pop around next Thursday... the day before I go we'll say our cheerios' then. I don't take kindly to railway platform or airport departure lounge goodbyes. They're too painful. A drink together the night before will do the trick for me... if that's okay with you."

"Sure is Charlie but I'll miss... well you know... stuff... talkin and that... like havin' a surrogate dad and just being around you."

Charlie cut me short, "For heaven's sake James don't start with the slobber now young man. Best leave it until next Thursday then you'll be able to tell me how much you love me and how you always have a picture of me in your head wearing a Basque and fishnet stockings."

We both laughed out loud at that conversation stopper.

"Now go home James and get your head around some of those other memories. They should come easier now. Look forward to the future and tackle those memories from the past and once you've done that don't look back."

I took my leave of Charlie that evening and did as he'd instructed. I headed for my flat in Glencoe Street with a new spring in my step. I was about to tackle memories of my pre-key-to-the-door years and beyond. That tenuous straddle between teenager, adult and real-life.

CHAPTER 16

With A Little Help From My Friends

$\blacksquare$

Those memories weren't as easy to sort out as I'd expected although I had a good old laugh at some of them. I couldn't figure out why most of them had stayed buried for so long. I began by sitting down and writing a list of my jobs after leaving school. That was a task in itself and I soon gave up when the list just grew and grew. I felt quite embarrassed as I remembered them in no particular order.

1) Bates Pit Trainee. Lasted four months. No way I was going to spend my days underground. I had a fear of confined spaces. I spent most of those months in the timber yard and on the Washer. First time I ever saw my dad naked in the showers and the last time I saw Scone Laidlaw and Terry Hall. Given a warning for smacking one of Scone's friends in the locker room. Scone was up for a fight but it didn't happen because Terry Hall talked him down. Didn't like warnings so I packed in.

2) R.D. Steedman, Antiquarian Bookseller. Grey Street Newcastle. Sacked after 2 months.

3) Orbit Chair Company. Lasted three months. Walked out one day because I was put on a job I didn't like. I had a strop, told the foreman he was a dick and never went back.

4) Arrow Construction. Lasted three months. Learned to drive my first fork-lift truck. Packed in for no reason.

5) Porter's Pipeworks. Lasted five months. I really liked that job and had a daily lift with Billy Armour. One day my head had one of its off days so I just decided to pack in.

6) Window cleaner lasted on and off for about a year... then got fed up and stopped. I'd initially gone canvassing with a lad called Chinny Nelson who'd worked with me at Orbit Chair Company. We were putting cards through peoples' doors offering our window cleaning services until Chinny happened to comment one day.

"Jimmy man we've got loads of people with our cards in their window."

"Aye... what's yer point Chinny?"

"We haven't got any ladders or buckets or anything."

"Aah've got a step-ladder."

"Is that cos you don't know who yer real ladder is?"

We both laughed at that but Chinny was like a dog with a bone, "We can't just keep piling customers up... not until we get some proper equipment."

"Chinny man that's just details."

Next day I waited for Chinny to turn up. He didn't. I was relieved really because I'd just dived into something without thinking it through. We had loads of customers but no means of cleaning their windows. I put the whole idea on the back burner for a few months. I still thought it may be a good idea but perhaps in future I should make sure I had the tools for the job. It would be a lot of years before I heard from Chinny again. I think he used to see me coming and then hide.

I stopped listing after job number eight or thereabouts. It was mortifying really because I was great at talking my way into a job but after having a head fuddle I quickly packed it in then went on a downer for a few weeks before going back to the dole office to see what was on offer. In those days you could walk into the dole office cum job centre and actually get a job. They were advertised on little cards on the big board in the dole office and they were all bona-fide work opportunities... or presumably so.

I must have been out of work for about 3 weeks. That was a long time for me because dole money was rubbish so I applied for a job with a Morpeth based outfit called Farm 2 Door a fruit and veg operation with door-to-door canvassing. It seemed to be a bit of a grind but nevertheless I got the job. Start day the following Monday.

The day I queued for my last dole-money payment there was a guy standing in line with me and he was humming away to himself and being very annoying. In those days the woman behind the counter would call out your name and you would step up to the grille sign your name then receive your dole money in cash. The giro days were still a few years off. Suddenly the payment lady gives a little snort... begins to titter then calls out a name... 'Rocky Marciano' and the whole of the queue in the dole office bursts out in gales of laughter. The annoying humming guy steps forward to collect his money and then swiftly leaves with head down whilst even the staff join in with us dole-queue attendees with hoots of merriment and huge guffaws. They would have been sacked nowadays but it was funny. I did feel sorry for Rocky though.

My next job with Farm 2 Door was to be an eye-opener for me in more ways than one. I was picked up in a covered wagon of a contraption outside of the Sidney Arms pub. My job training didn't even last the half-an-hour that it took the wagon to transport us to a private housing estate in Whitley Bay.

My job that day was to knock on doors and ask the resident if they would like to buy a four-stone bag of potatoes. We had a ton and a half in the back of the wagon. Sixty bags of potatoes to sell. Roger the driver was the boss and did nothing else but drive and collect the cash from us when we made a sale. He sat there smoking and eating sandwiches all day and only moving when the lorry needed shifting into the next street. The lad working with me was called Albert and he was the dumbest lad I'd ever met. I'm not doing the conceited Grammar school thing... because we all have different layers of intelligence and different skills... all apart from Albert. Poor Albert pre-dated Forrest Gump by decades but that comparison is the closest I can get to describing him. Not that I ever bought him a box of chocolates or anything. I actually liked him and we gelled okay but the obnoxious way he was spoken to and shouted at by Roger was akin to mental cruelty.

The potatoes were nine shillings for a four-stone bag but Roger encouraged us to increase the price if the homeowner seemed like an easy mark. Each bag I sold at the nine-shilling mark earned me one-and-sixpence with Roger taking the rest. Any sold at an increased price and the extra was supposed to be shared fifty-fifty with Roger. I realised we were engaged in some sort of a con when Roger told me that I had to stress to the homeowner that our produce was regulated and approved by the potato marketing board.

I followed Albert around as he did his first half-dozen knocks just so I could get a feel for the patter being used. Albert unfortunately didn't have any worthwhile sales technique. Knock-knock-knock...

"Yes?"

"D'yer want some taties missus?"

"Pardon me?"

"Taties in a big bag... canny cheap?"

"No thank you."

"Okay ta'." Then on to the next door. I realised pretty quickly that I wouldn't be earning much money using Albert's sales pitch so after another few doors I headed back to the wagon.

"Roger... what kind of taties are we selling?"

"Pentland Dell... that's what we've got today. I only buy them or Maris Piper cos they're good chippers."

"Are they straight off the farm?"

"Course they are." I knew that was a lie.

"How cheap is nine bob?"

"Not sure kid... but I think it's less than half the price you would pay if you were buying them by the pound. Why?"

"So that I've got something to say at the doors instead of 'want some taties in a big bag'... cos it's not very inviting is it."

"Aye... Albert is as thick as pig shit but he keeps plodding on."

I realised then that I didn't like Roger. He'd used the TAPS and I wasn't impressed with that. Albert wasn't bright but it was him out in the street knocking on doors while Roger sat reading his newspaper and being hacky-lazy. Time for Batesy to swing into action.

I began working the other side of the street to Albert. I approached my first door. Knock-knock-knock.

Door opens, "Yes?"

"Ohh hello, sorry to disturb you missus. I'm from Highbarns Farm. We're delivering four-stone bags of Pentland Dell potatoes to some of your neighbours and they're the first of the main crop. Fortunately we've ended up with a few spare bags. They're brilliant chippers. If you'd like one we can let you have one for eleven bob which is less than half the price you'd pay buying them by the pound. And they're Potato Marketing Board approved of course."

Lady seemed impressed, "Ohh... that sounds ideal. How many do you have?"

I make up a number, "I think we have four left."

She gives it some thought, "Ermmm... well I hope you don't think I'm being cheeky but is there any way you could let me have two? I'm sure my sister would like one as well but you won't catch her in because she's at work."

I pretended to think about it for a few seconds. "All right missus but keep it under your hat cos it's supposed to be one per house."

She gave a big grin and a wink, "Aye that'll be right. Wait there and I'll get the money for you."

"Actually missus I'll just go and get the taties for you while you're sorting out the cash."

I wasn't eighteen yet and those bags were heavy but I carried both bags into the woman's kitchen. She handed over two ten bob notes and three shillings.

If nothing else I'm an honest lad, "You've given me too much missus," I said and tried to hand her a shilling back."

"You keep it son... it's a tip. It's a godsend really because I won't have to carry taties back from the greengrocers'. I always end up with one arm longer than the other," Then she paused and smiled. "I don't suppose you could let next-door have one as well. I've just been telling her about them over the back fence and she would like a bag."

This lark was becoming very lucrative. One house... three bags. I was grinning like a Cheshire cat.

That first call kick-started my potato career which was to last for the next three or so weeks. I quickly sorted out a plan of action and I asked Albert to stop knocking on doors because his sales technique was wasting potential customers. He was a big friendly lump of a lad and we began to work it between us. I would do the knocking, talking and selling and Albert would do the carrying and delivering. If anyone happened to ask Albert about the price I'd primed him to respond with 'don't know... I just do the carrying'. The deal was that Albert would be paid ninepence for every bag that I sold and that he carried. He was happy with that. It was more money than he'd been earning. He told me that sometimes he worked all day for as little as ten-bob. As for myself I was selling the bags for two-bob more than Roger expected and with him sitting in the cab all day he wasn't about to find out as long as I told him about the occasional bag sold at top whack.

By four-o-clock that day we'd emptied the lorry. Not a single bag of taties left. Roger was amazed. We settled up the cash. Albert and I both ended up with Two pounds and five shillings and Albert was chuffed to bits. I of course had a further five and a half quid in my jeans pocket because we'd sold every single bag for eleven shillings instead of nine and Roger was none the wiser apart from the few extra money sales I'd told him about. It may have been a little dodgy on my part but you know what... I couldn't care less.

I slipped Albert an extra five-bob and told him it was a thank you for doing all the heavy lifting because it was so important and we couldn't have done it without him. Albert became my friend that day. Quite honestly he seemed to be so overwhelmed because someone was treating him like a normal human-being. He seemed pretty shocked that someone was giving him a gift that wasn't expected. I don't think that anyone had ever given that lad anything in his life other than ridicule.

That was some day's work and extremely lucrative. I was absolutely knackered but looking forward to tomorrow's day of graft. Onwards and upwards as my history teacher Mr Rowland used to say... in Latin of course 'Porro et sursum', but nevertheless I was on to a big earner here and long may it continue.

"What time are you picking me up tomorrow Roger."

"Not tomorrow son I've got to sign on."

"Ehhh?"

"Sign on man... the dole."

"But... is this not a proper job?"

"Divvent be daft man we'll only have three or four more weeks on the taties. Then me and Albert will be back on the scrap. Fill yer boots for a few weeks Jim," then he frowned and asked, "Ye haven't gone and signed off have ye?"

"Aye of course... it was on the proper jobs board in the dole. I've even got me cards to give ye for my stamp."

"Stamp be buggered... get real man Jim. Ye've got to learn how to play the system. Get yersell back doon to the dole tomorrow and tell them I didn't turn up. Ye'll probably only lose one day. If they phone our house I'll get wor lass to say the lorry broke down and I've got the flu or something and we couldn't get in touch with you because you haven't get a phone number. I'll pick ye up on Wednesday same time same place and we'll have a crack at the new estate in Cramlington."

We drove back to Blyth in silence and he dropped me off outside Cowpen Club. I walked home from there.

Now I had a problem. I couldn't tell mam it wasn't a proper job after having told her that it was. She'd think I'd been lying one way or another. And I certainly couldn't tell her that I wouldn't be at work on my second day because she'd immediately be suspicious. So I said nothing to arouse any awkward questions.

"What was your first day like?" she asked as I sat eating my tea.

"All right."

"What did you have to do?"

"Just loading up from farms then unloading at the other end at the Team Valley." That seemed a decent response.

"Have you got a week lying on." I thought I'd get a question about the money. Mam would be expecting her board money and wanted to know if she'd have to wait a fortnight for it.

"Ermmm... I'm not sure cos I didn't like to ask on my first day but the lad I was working with says he got paid on his first week."

"Aye well if you do make sure you don't have it spent before you pay your board." She paused. "Do you need bait putting up for tomorrow?"

"Aye... just a few sandwiches. It's canny heavy work."

"Pfff... you young-un's don't know the meaning of heavy work." That was the end of the conversation. Because of Roger's dole confession I now I had to plan an awayday where I wouldn't be spotted. I was hoping for a sunny day. But first I had to brave the dole.

I was contrite and apologetic when I presented myself to re-sign at the dole office the following day. I gave them the facts as presented to me by Roger and as expected they made a follow up phone call. Roger's wife must have stuck to the script because I received a half-hearted apology from the counter lass. Sorry that I'd been sent on a wild-goose chase. They signed me back on the social again with the welcome comment that there should be no break in my dole money as it hadn't been my fault.

After the dole I took myself and my sandwiches for a leisurely stroll down to the beach and then on along the sands all the way to Seaton Sluice. They actually served me in the Ship hotel and I had a furtive pint of beer and a cheese toastie. I hung around the harbour for a few hours.

I eventually finished off the sandwiches before taking a bus back to Blyth. I arrived home around about the time I would have finished work and all was hunky-dory. Job done.

Then Cramlington happened and with it the end of my naivety and innocence.

To be absolutely honest my love life or girl-friend life had been somewhat sparse up to that point. I'd embarked on several on-off stop-start flirtations. I'd negotiated a few fumbles and furtive gropes which had furthered my romantic education not one iota. I found I could attract girlfriends... with my being so incredibly arresting and irresistible but the problem was that once I got a lass I didn't know what to do with her. All that physical stuff was still a mystery to me. I'd even read the Kinsey Report and Kama Sutra but neither of them gave you the real instruction manual... you know... like 'first you put your tongue in the girl's ear and waggle it around... then when she moans you smack her hard on the bum with a stick of rhubarb'. There was none of that. In fact all of the folk in the Kama Sutra seemed to have more arms and legs than normal and for some reason they were all exceedingly bendy. There was no instruction as to what to do when this happens and what to do when that happens. So being seventeen and still girl ignorant I just hadn't bothered for a while. I mean... I still rushed to read mam's Freeman's catalogue whenever it was delivered and would barricade myself in my room to peruse the women's underwear photo's... but that was about the pinnacle of my extracurricular activities.

That Wednesday was to be an eye-opener for me. I had no idea what was in store when Roger picked me up from the usual place and I certainly didn't expect to be showing anything other than my spuds.

Roger was in a jovial mood as we motored towards the new Cramlington housing estate. He was whistling away to himself and to be fair he was really good at it. He was whistling 'Mairzy-Doats' and I quite liked that cos I'd heard my mam humming it. I was feeling enthused myself because I'd been doing the calculations and if I could carry on selling at the same rate as I had on Monday I'd make myself a good enough wedge to be able to afford a set of ladders and other equipment to set up my window business.

Albert wasn't too happy though. I didn't speak and I gave him some space at first but nevertheless he just seemed to be on a downer so eventually I asked him why he was down in the dumps.

"Cos I've been thinking." He said.

"Thinking?"

"Aye."

"Maybe best not to do too much of that then Albert... you'll end up bruising your brain."

"Will I?"

"No of course not... but what's the matter with you."

"Don't like these houses."

"What?"

"Don't like these new houses we're going to."

Roger chipped in as he drove. "Take no notice of daft lad Jim. He just doesn't want to bump into the naughty wifey again that fancied him when we were here last time."

The wife that fancied Albert? Now that statement was intriguing. No offence intended but how desperate was she?

"She were right rude," Albert protested.

"She just wanted to be friendly Albert... she liked you." Roger chuckled.

"She were still rude. Me mam would go daft if she knew I'd been in a house with a woman walking around with her busters out... and she smacked my bum without asking."

I couldn't help laughing and Roger was absolutely howling but poor Albert was angry and on the verge of tears. I put a lid on the laughter and said, "Don't worry about it Albert I'll do the house and then you won't need to go anywhere near it."

"But what if you sell her some taties... I'll have to carry them into her house and she might start showing her busters off again."

I was struggling manfully to keep a straight face, "I'll carry them myself Albert if I sell her some taties and I'll still give you your ninepence."

That calmed him down and the atmosphere became bearable again. Ten minutes later and Roger had pulled up in a close. There was still building work going on behind this collection of houses. They were all Leech new builds. We sat for a while smoking in the cab while we decided on a plan of action. Roger only had fifty bags of taties today. That was a disappointment because I now had a quid less to aim for.

"Howay then Albert we won't make our fortune sitting on our backsides," I gave Albert an elbow dig, "Time to motor."

We jumped out of the truck. "Which is Bessie Buster's house?" I asked.

Albert looked sheepish. "It's not in this street, it's over the other side," he replied, pointing to some houses in the distance.

We cracked on and it was brilliant. Almost every house where there was someone in clicked up a sale of today's offering... Maris Piper. My head was awash with calculations. I was making money hand over fist. Albert was grafting away manfully with all the heavy lifting but he must have been exhausted because the taties were selling like hot cakes and he was constantly back and forward with a sack on his back. In three hours or less we were down to our last few bags as we pulled into a cul-de-sac type of street. Albert wasn't happy and I immediately knew why.

I asked, "Is this the Bessie street Albert?"

"Aye."

"Which one is it?"

"Ower there," he said, pointing with his head.

"Which one?"

"Straight ower last one on the right."

"Stop looking so worried Albert man. I'll sell those last bags before I come to that house."

I didn't quite manage to do that. Unfortunately Albert didn't know his left from his right. So with one bag left to sell and still 3 houses away from where I thought Albert's fancy lady lived I knocked on a door... last one on the left.

After a few seconds the door opened a fraction and a head appeared with the rest of the body still behind the door. It was an attractive looking lady and she gave me a questioning smile.

"Yes?"

I began with my sales pitch. Sorry to disturb you miss but we're delivering local farm produce to some of your neighbours..."

At that point she interrupted as I knew she would, "It's Mrs."

That line was one of the hooks I used. Now for the winding in of the reel. "Sorry about that... you don't look old enough to be married, I thought you must be the daughter." She looked about thirty but she knew sales patter when she heard it. She grinned.

"Would you like to come in? I've just been in the shower and I don't want to stand at the door."

"Okay."

She opened the door and stepped into the centre of the passageway. My eyes popped out on stalks. She was wearing some sort of negligee thing but it was completely see-through. I didn't know whether to look up... down or away and there was distinct movement in the nether region.

"My window was open and I heard you talking to Lisa in the corner house about your potatoes," she said. "I'd be very interested in your potatoes.?" I was seventeen years old but at that moment I felt about twelve.

"I ermmm... they're Maris Piper."

She gave a giggly laugh as she brushed past me and shut the front door. She smelt freshly showered. "Well you've definitely made another sale," then she took my hand and squeezed, "Follow me and I'll show you where to put your Maris Piper," then she led me into the sitting room.

Half an hour later I climbed back into the truck after delivering the final bag. They'd been waiting for me to reappear and that came as a relief because I thought they might have been fed up and decided to go home. I'd been as quick as I could... too quick I'd been reliably informed. There was no comment from Roger or Albert. Complete silence. That suited me.

Roger started the truck up and backed out past a few parked cars. After we'd left the estate the only thing that Roger said was, "Hope you got paid for that last bag."

"Aye... I did."

"Good... we'll settle up when I drop you off."

Albert sat quietly for a little while but then seemed unable to contain himself and asked. "Why did you go to that woman's house?"

"Why Albert?... Cos you told me wrong man."

"No I didn't."

"Yes you did... cos you don't know your left from your right."

"Yes I do,"

"No Albert you don't... you told me it was last house on the right but it was last house on the left."

He grinned triumphantly, "Aye, but if I turned around it would be right cos it changes when you turn right around."

"Ehhh?"

"Sorry for telling you wrong but it's just that when you turn around... you know like backwards... then left and right change over. So I told you proper but I just got mixed up with my front and back."

I hadn't the foggiest what he was on about so I let it lie.

Then Albert asked sheepishly, "Did that rude woman show you her busters?"

I'd hoped that my dalliance wouldn't become a topic of conversation and Roger had very sensibly kept his own counsel but Albert didn't have that same inhibitor mechanism.

"Aye Albert she did... all three of them."

Albert was still wrestling with that statement when I was dropped off right outside my front door. We'd settled up the cash but Roger didn't know that I'd been paid £5 for that final bag of taties with the promise of more of the same the next time we were in the area. Tomorrow however we would be working Gosforth... it seemed promising. Strangely, when I undressed that night I discovered that I was wearing y-backs... somehow I'd put my undies on the wrong way round.

All in all we had a cracking three and a half weeks before it came to an end. Roger I'll always remember as a bit of a fly-by-night character who knew how to manipulate the system but I'll remember Albert with affection. He was a harmless soul. We would meet up again in 1989 quite by accident and he'd work on my book business for a few weeks before we finally lost contact. I hope he lived a good life.

The cash from those weeks was enough to kit out my window-cleaning enterprise. So onwards and upwards... literally for this budding entrepreneur. I'll remember that interlude mainly though as the time when my growing-up education was fast-tracked by an obliging bored housewife whose name was... ermmm... can't remember!... Ohhh aye... and pigs might fly!

CHAPTER 17

My Sharona

––––––––––––––––––––■––––––––––––––––––––

Ashington hospital 18th August 1970 and I'm nineteen, married and terrified because a nurse is gowning me up to go into a delivery room to witness the birth of our child. I really don't want to do it. I mean... howay let's get real here cos it's not the natural way is it? Sheila my wife is in the delivery room... cos she has no option and that's as it should be. But let's be honest about this because since time immemorial it's been the women's job to do the baby stuff... you know? all the belly-button carry-on... the shrieking and swearing and the squelchy things. It's the blokes' jobs to do the hard graft with the cigars and to brave the pub for the wetting of the baby's head... cos that's the natural order handed down through the generations.

But for some reason on this occasion the nurse is insistent and protest is going to get me nowhere and there's no backing out. The nurse is telling me how all new men are at their child's birth... ehhh? New men? What about old men? I quite fancy being one of those if it will get me out of this gown thing. How on earth has this state of affairs come about? Well I'll tell you.... if you'll lend me your ear and believe what I'm about to say... Yes?... then listen up.

The number six bus has just left Newcastle and it's heading for Blyth as its final destination. I've just finished another day at college. Now that I'm no longer at school and at my mother's insistence I'm doing a fast-track maths course so that I can re-sit my maths 'O' level at some point... the one that I failed last year. My potato interlude ended a fortnight ago and I've had to put my window-cleaning business on hold until I complete this three-week crammer.

I'm sitting in the bus on my own... minding my own business but behind me are two of the loudest lasses you will ever hear. After my Maris Piper experience in Cramlington I seem to have acquired a certain allure but it's embarrassing and I don't really understand it. This is the third day in a row the lasses have sat in the seat behind me and I'm under no illusions that their comments are aimed at me. I'm really still quite shy and this new-found attracting girls thing makes me feel uneasy. I still find talking to girls a difficult exercise especially if they're bonny and then I become incredibly shy and tongue-tied so most of the time I just don't bother.

I'm sitting pretending to read my Chronicle as I hear the opening salvo from the two lasses behind me. "Dear Cathy and Claire, I see this really gorgeous lad on the bus every evening but he doesn't notice me." They were pretend reading from the problem page in their 'Jackie' magazine and being uber loud and giggly. "Do you think I should just go and sit on his knee and give him a big sloppy kiss?" Other passengers were having a chuckle at these two loud lasses and at my expense. I wasn't liking it.

"Dear Cathy and Claire, do you think I should buy the dreamboat a present? I keep dreaming about him walking around the bedroom wearing his silk jim-jams?" Now everyone on the bus seemed to be snorting, giggling and having a jolly whilst I shrank further into my shell. I was embarrassed and praying that Annitsford would turn up quickly so that these two nightmares would get off the bus. I'd just reached the dizzy heights of six-foot tall but the louder these two became the more I shortened. Hunched over in my seat I now felt about four-foot six.

Then someone sat down beside me. It was a lass... I knew that because I'd seen the legs sticking out of the short skirt as she sat down. I hadn't looked at the face in case she made eye contact and I fixed my gaze out of the bus window and pretended not to notice that I'd been joined.

"Thought I'd come and rescue you... from your fan club," the girl chuckled and I thought I recognised the voice. I turned to look at the face and felt a huge sense of relief. I'd been saved by Linda Winter a bonny lass from Hallside who'd been in the year below me at school.

I mouthed 'thank you' as the comments from behind me dried up completely.

"So what time are you picking me up tonight," Linda asked in a loud voice to leave the two 'Jackie' comedians in no doubt that their prey was in fact someone's boyfriend.

"Half-seven."

"Right I'll be ready... are we going out on the motorbike?"

She had me chuckling because she was really hamming it up. "Yeh okay, we'll have a spin out to Whitley."

"I'll tell my dad not to wait up ehhh?" Then she linked arms and put a head on my shoulder leaving those two lassies in no doubt that they needed to look elsewhere for their sport. I was relieved and shortly afterwards they alighted as per usual outside the Bridge Inn at Annitsford.

When they'd gone we gave up on the pretence and the arm linking and just chatted away until the bus reached our stop on Cowpen Road. I had no problem chatting with Linda even though she was gorgeous because I realised we'd just been pretending and she wasn't really interested in me. I walked Linda most of the way home and we took leave of each other on Tynedale with a big smile and wave. I'll always be grateful for the emotional rescue that day.

Life moved on apace after that and I concentrated my efforts on my new window-cleaning business. I lost my shyness too and now my hair was long and thick. I'd morphed into a kind of Keith Richards but obviously better looking and it seemed to give me much more confidence with the fair sex. Several girl-friends came and went during those next few months one of whom was none other than one of the 'Jackie' lasses from Annitsford.

That interlude lasted a matter of weeks during which time she thought I had a Lambretta scooter and I was also the lead singer with a band called 'Tug and the Catslappers'... don't ask how that name was thought up. Well you can actually... it was Titch Irving who thought of the 'Catslappers' and I added the 'Tug' as lead singer.

Titch and I had bumped into each other on the day that a procession of Scottish mods zoomed through Blyth town centre on their Lambrettas and Vespas. All the bad mod/rocker confrontations had more or less fizzled out by 1966 but not in Glasgow for some reason. This was 1968 and more than a dozen of those Scots mods on their scooters and most with regulation fish-tail parkas whizzed down Waterloo Road and Bridge Street honking horns as they did so. The entire town seemed to stand still and gawp at the spectacle including myself because on the back of one of the scooters was my old pal Sid. We hadn't seen each other for a few years now but he spotted me in the static crowd as the convoy flashed past and he gave a thumbs up salute.

I felt a tap on the shoulder and turned. "Thought it was you," said Titch Irving with a big grin on his face.

"Hi Titch... long-time no see. How are you doing?"

"Canny man."

"Where ye grafting?"

"Aahmm carpet fitting. What about you?"

"Window cleaning... I thought ye were gonna join up?"

"I am... soon."

"So do you know what that was aall about Titch... the march of the mods?"

"Word is they've come down from Scotland lookin' for rockers and they've joined up with a few of the Morpeth lads. Can't see them finding many rockers outside the Jubilee café can you."

"Is that where they're heading?"

"Aye apparently... they must think Blyth beach is like Clacton or Margate or something. They'll probably end up knockin' some old bloke off his pushbike and calling it the battle of Gloucester Lodge or something."

Titch hadn't changed. He was still a card and a half.

"Number eight bus is about to leave. Fancy a run along to the beach?"

"Aye okay."

We ran together to catch the bus.

"Remember Titch... we like the Who and Small Faces."

"Ehhh... who on earth would like Happy Jack?" He grimaced.

"Aye that was a bit of a car crash. But I think they were just tryin' to do something silly like Yellow Submarine."

"Let's hope they don't do any sillier stuff cos that one's cack."

"Okay... remember we're both mods though."

Ten minutes later and we're getting off the bus at second beach. Sure enough the Scot mods were here and their scooters were parked up in a long gleaming row beside the café. Sid was with the gang of mods and he spied us from a distance but made no move to come and greet us or even acknowledge us. Perhaps we didn't look hip enough because I could see that Sid was wearing a smart suit with a highwayman collar under his now open parka. Titch and I were just in jeans and brushed denim jackets... obviously not mod enough.

We forgot about Sid and the cold-shoulder. He obviously had a new load of friends to impress. Titch and I sat down on the grass beside the concrete ship and lit up a couple of tabs.

A few minutes later and it was Titch who noticed two girls approaching us... he gave me a nudge, pointed with his head and winked. "Let me do the talking... you follow my lead."

"Nee daft stuff Titch."

"Aye as if." He grinned.

"Hiya," grinned the taller of the two girls as they came to a halt in front of us, "Are you with the mods?"

I kept quiet as instructed, "Nah," said Titch, "We were... but then we had to disappoint them and they aren't happy about it. They thought we were going to be playing at the Mayfair this weekend but our next booking's not for another fortnight."

The lasses seemed surprised. They been ready to head off towards the Scotch mods but they stopped dead in their tracks and looked us up and down, "Playing what... are you in a proper group or something?"

There was no holding Titch back now, "Aye, aahh thought that's why you'd come across to talk... for autographs an' that. Anyways... yes we're in a group. We played the Sands club for three nights last week. Just got our first recording contract with Decca."

"Naah, you're having me on."

Titch just shrugged and looked away, "All right... please yersell."

"You're serious aren't you... about the group and stuff?"

"Yeh of course... we were on the cover of 'London Scene' mag a fortnight ago, 'the Catslappers."

I could barely keep my laugh in so I jumped in before Titch hammed it up too much. "Tug and the Catslappers' is our full title. I'm Tug Thomson the lead singer... and this is

Gravy Browning," I gave a flourish to introduce Titch, "And he plays the triangle and the kazoo." I don't know why I'd came out with that load of rubbish.

Titch was looking daggers at me so I grinned at the girls, "Only kidding of course Gravy is our drummer... a bit like in the style of Keith Moon... wild and talented." The little wind up was turning into a big lie but the girls hadn't turned a hair when I'd named Titch as Gravy Browning.

"You're both a bit young to be in a band," said the big lass.

"Talent doesn't have age limits," Titch replied confidently.

"Wow," said the smaller girl who hadn't spoken yet and she was looking at Titch Gravy with cow eyes. Titch wasn't about to miss a trick and he stood up, walked up to the girl and took her hand. He'd found a lass his own height and she was starstruck.

"We're just having a day off from rehearsals and the recording studio. Our single is out next month and our manager reckons it's going to be big."

"Wow... what's it called? Asked Titch's lass."

No hesitation from Gravy, "It's called Down the Hairpin... and the B-side is called No Brakes Today," Titch was laying it on with a trowel. "D'yer fancy a walk over to the sand dunes and I'll tell you all about it."

The lass grinned, nodded and off they went.

We watched Titch and the girl as they headed for the dunes, "Your drummer doesn't waste any time does he?" said the taller lass then she gave me a hard stare, "I've seen you somewhere before... I'm sure of it."

I'd recognised her almost immediately as being the loud 'Jackie' lass from the bus. No point avoiding it so I said, "I'm the lad you sat behind and gave so much grief to on the number six bus."

"Ohhh aye... that's where... ermmm sorry about that we were only having a bit of fun," she eked out a weak laugh. "Where's the girlfriend today?"

"It wasn't my girlfriend she just decided to save me from you two."

"Aahh right... sorry again. So what were you doing on the bus if you've got a motorbike?"

"It's a scooter and you don't leave a fancy scooter with all the mirrors and bits and bobs standing around in Newcastle. We were rehearsing."

"During the day?"

"Well you can't rehearse at the Mayfair on an evening when there's acts on."

"Oh aye... course not."

"So where's your scooter?"

"We didn't bring it today because we thought there'd be trouble and I've spent too much money on it for it to be wrecked. Anyway it's going into the garage on Monday for some chrome work."

She accepted that, "So no girlfriend then?"

"Not at the minute."

"Play your cards right and you could have one."

"Is that right?"

"Aye... d'yer live in Blyth?"

"Yeh... not far away."

"So we could go to yours and talk about it." She was being very forward.

That was unexpected and I needed a get-out, "Can't go to mine because my dad would go daft. He's a copper. A sergeant and we live in a police house and we're not allowed to have girlfriends in a constabulary building. It's a bit of a bummer but the group will be off to London soon so I'll be out of there." I was thinking on the fly now.

"So I'm a girlfriend am I?"

"Could be if ye play your cards right."

She gave a huge smile, "So do you fancy giving me a guided tour of the sand dunes instead?"

Indeed I did. We headed off in the same direction as Titch.

It was two weeks later and I felt really bad that Saturday evening as I stood and watched the bus disgorging passengers at the Haymarket. Sally Sand-dune as I'd nicknamed her was herding a group of pals as they alighted from the United bus. There must have been about a dozen of them and I watched from a tobacconist shop doorway as the giggling crowd began to head off in the direction of their evening destination... the Mayfair. I'd hoped beyond hope that I'd be able to think of some excuse to make them give up this evening's trek to see Sally Sand-dune's fella belting out a repertoire of songs with supergroup 'Tug and the Catslappers', surely they must have read through their Jackie magazine or Rave and other teen mags and found there wasn't a single mention of the band. It seemed not.

I was feeling wretched as I took the bus back home. Those small lies that had been spontaneously thought up for a bit of a laugh had taken on a life of their own and now everything was about to blow up and disappoint some nice people. Sally Sand-dune had turned out to be a nice lass and she'd introduced me to her parents which made it even worse because they were nice too and I hadn't the guts to put a halt to the lie and tell them the truth. Her dad had bought me a pint in the Bridge Inn and introduced me as a musician and I'd even signed two autographs as 'Tug Thomson' for a couple of his closest pals. Those people were all going to feel so foolish and used. Not as foolish as me of course because after tonight I'd have to dye my hair and wear a false moustache or something. Alternatively I could of course just lie low for a few months and dodge the moustache thing.

I imagined the look of incredulity on the face of the Mayfair doorman as the excited girls asked, "What time are Tug and the Catslappers playing cos we know Tug and Gravy?" Oh dear what a thoroughly awful thing Titch and I had done. This evening was going to end up with a bevy of sad and disillusioned young ladies feeling like absolute idiots.

I didn't expect that they'd come looking for us... myself and Titch because they'd quickly realise that we'd been feeding them a line. I certainly couldn't imagine they'd come looking for a lad called Gravy Browning or indeed trawl the police houses for Tug Thomson and his police force dad.

For a long time afterwards if I needed to go to Newcastle I would take the number 8 bus and head off around the coast road route instead of taking the shorter journey via the number six route which passed through Annitsford. I was never to see Sally Sand-dune again. I did hear however that she'd put me out of her mind and married a farmer.

Titch and I met up the next day. Both of us felt somewhat contrite but we were having a joke about it nonetheless.

"Ye nearly got us caught out on that big lie Titch?... I didn't know what to say when she kept asking questions about the recording contract with Decca."

"Did ye tell her I meant Decca Raisbeck?" We both laughed at that one.

"Anyway what was your thing aall about Jim... with you telling her you were called Terry?"

"It was cos she asked why I was called Tug and I just thought of the first name that came into my head beginning with a 't' and told her it was Terry. I said Tug had been my nickname from schooldays. Anyway how did you explain the 'Gravy' Browning?"

"Same as you. I said Browning was my surname and Gravy was my nickname for obvious reasons. She thinks my proper name is Gary."

We both laughed. We were sitting under the shade of a tree in Ridley Park with two cans each of McEwan's Export to keep us company. It was pointless trying to wheedle our way into a pub because Titch would never be served even though he was older than myself. We were a little wary about going down to the beach in case we were being searched for by the girls... and maybe their big brothers so we sat there smoking and drinking for a while and the Export was weaving its magic.

It was a nice day... not too hot but the sun was out. We chattered away about all sorts as we sat there smoking and drinking. Then we went quiet and Titch seemed to be miles away for a minute or two before giving an inebriated snort and saying, "Can ye imagine if Sand-dune Sally was a Geordie Twinkle and she was singin' about ye Jim." Tich started tapping out time on his jeans like a drummer and then burst into silly song.

"But it's too late to give that bloke me love tonight."

"Please wait at the gates of Mayfair for me... Te-erry."

"He rode into the night (da-da-da-da)

"Peddlin' off on his owld pushbi-i-ike."

"I cried to him in fright."

"For fuck's sake man Terry ya chain's off."

We laughed so much at that one. It didn't even scan properly. It was plain and utter stupidity and so ridiculous that we chortled away like a pair of halfwits. That was Titch at his most creative and on intoxicated top form. Then an old woman appeared in front of us.

"You lads are disgusting. Using filthy language like that when there's so many bairns over there and in the paddling pool." She was pointing towards a gaggle of children and mothers who had overheard Titch's raucous offering. Titch and I looked at each other and we should have been apologetic but instead we started giggling. We jumped up and made a run for it carrying our opened beer cans with Export slopping out as we sprinted from the park. We were both seventeen but we legged it like a pair of ten-year-olds who'd just been spotted scrumping crab apples.

That would be the last day I spent with Titch. I'd see him several years later in Newcastle. He was in his army uniform and I was happy for him but I was in a rush that day and didn't have time to say anything but 'hi' and something like "We'll have to meet up for a pint Titch." I regret not having had the time to have a bit of a chinwag... because I didn't know it at the time but I wouldn't have the opportunity again.

Then came that fateful New Year. It was my first New Year doing proper first-footing. I wasn't eighteen for months yet but I'd got a half-bottle of whisky in one pocket and a piece of coal and a little bag of salt in another. That's what the big folk did so I was going to do that too.

The midnight bells of course had to be welcomed in at home with some tall dark and handsome bloke being the first-foot if you could manage to find one. If you happened to look out of your window at a minute to midnight you'd see all the husbands standing outside their front doors with their lumps of coal and sundry new year offerings in hand... and all looking sheepish. My dad was our first-foot that year... send him out of the back door at two minutes to twelve and welcome him in through the front door two minutes later... "Eeeh I've never seen you since last year," silly but nice.

I was allowed beer now even though dad was looking forward to my turning eighteen so he could join me up at the club... either the Duke of Wellington or Cowpen Club then I could become officially affiliated. The clock struck twelve... mam let dad in and we all joined hands and did the 'Old Acquaintance' thing. Then dad went through the time-honoured speech with the health, wealth and happiness and may all your troubles be little ones and may the best day of last year be the worst day of this new year. Job's a good un'.

Then when home duty was done I took off to visit the old Axwell stomping ground. I was hoping I'd be made welcome at the houses I'd marked down as possibilities. It turned out I was and I made brief stops at Harry and Mary Thomson's and then Sylvia Connor's and on to the Fowler's house before heading for Leeches estate and Swaledale. I was off to the Potter house. I'd bumped into Alan the week before and he'd told me to call in if I was out and about at New Year. That was an invitation I couldn't turn down.

Tynedale Drive sometime after 1.00 am. I'm ambling along on my own and there's a bunch of young females approaching me. I sort of know what's about to happen.

"Happy New Year," seemed to spring from four female throats all at the same time. Then I was leaped on. Four passionate kisses later and I'm left holding the last of the kissers.

"Knew ye'd be a good kisser," said the grinning face. I have to shut one eye to focus because I've drank far too much.

Then I realised who I was holding on to, "Sheila Potter... what are you doing out? You should be in bed."

"Well Jim Bates... thanks for the offer but I'm off to a party... where are you going?"

"Your house."

"Good luck it's chocker."

To this day I still don't know why I asked but I said, "I'm off to watch the Spartans tomorrow if you want to come."

There was no hesitation, "Aye all right... what time?"

"Three o'clock kick off."

"What's your address?"

"Fourteen Hortondale."

"I'll come to yours about two-ish."

"Aye okay... Happy New Year." Then a lot of grins and waves as the lasses departed on their giggly way and I was off to the Potter house in Swaledale. I'd forgotten within minutes the arrangements I'd just made for the Spartans' match. The rest of that evening was just a blur and I can't remember how I made it home but I must have... because.

New Year's Day afternoon. Knock-knock-knock on my bedroom door, "Jim will ye wake yourself up there's a lass at the door wanting to go to football or something."

"Urrrggghhhh... what?"

"Harry Potter's lassie. She says you're going to the football together."

"Tell her I've got the flu or something mam. I'm dying."

"Aye well ye shouldn't drink what the big lads drink. Don't be making daft arrangements again... it's embarrassing." Then she went off to pass on the 'he's not well pet... clinging to life by his fingertips' message. I rolled over and went back to sleep.

I surfaced about four o'clock. Tea time that day was a little later than usual, around about sixish because dad had been late coming back from 'the Duke'. The table as usual was groaning with all the baked offerings adorning the table. Strangely enough I'd woken up completely sober and I had a monster of an appetite. I'd skipped dinner-time but now I wasn't feeling remotely nauseous and I was hoying ham and egg flan and sausage rolls into my mouth like there was no tomorrow.

Knock-knock-knock at the front door.

"I'll get it," says my sister Ann and jumps up to answer the knock.

Voices at the door... then a few moments later Ann is back in the kitchen with Sheila Potter in tow. "Make some room for another chair Billy," she says to my nephew who jumps up and scrapes his chair along to create a space. Billy is a good-looking kid of seven by now and no-longer resembles a monkey although we're still a little wary when taking him anywhere near trees. Ann brings a spare chair through from the dining room. Sheila sits down looking decidedly embarrassed.

It's time for me to do the 'knight in shining armour' routine. I'm just pleased that all the sandwiches have been cut diagonal instead of straight across the middle. It gives the table a posh ambience.

"Okay everyone this is Sheila... a friend and also sister of Alan Potter." Some murmurs of welcome from the gathering. "Sheila this is everyone," I say and then introduce the family individually.

"Well get the lass a cup," says mam, "or a glass... Eeeh man what's he like? Ye'd think he'd been brought up with nee manners." It was a surprise to hear my mam being welcoming to a lass. Usually it would be 'she's ower young' or 'could ye not have picked one who doesn't look like Ena Sharples?' However she seemed to warm to Sheila immediately... and we weren't an item or even dating... just a chance meeting and a daft football invitation.

That would all change of course because here I am almost 2 years later wearing a gown and a plastic hat thing to keep my profusion of hair in control and I'm awaiting my date with destiny outside Ashington Hospital delivery room. Fortunately the big fella up in the sky takes pity on me and sends a nurse out of the delivery room to tell me, "Really sorry James but we're going to have to disappoint you. You're going to have to wait out here. There's nothing to worry about but Sheila is having difficulty birthing naturally. We're going to have to do a 'C' section... but everything is going to be fine. Find yourself a seat in the waiting room." Then in an eye blink she's gone.

So I'm sitting in a waiting room with Sheila's dad and slightly worried now. I'm wondering what a 'C' section is. Isn't that the bit of an orchestra that play the brass instruments? Surely they can't have musicians in there. If they have then they'd all better be wearing blindfolds. I don't want to kick off and have a confrontation with a bloke and his flugelhorn.

Two hours or so later and I'm looking through a window into the baby room. I've been told that I am now the proud father of a beautiful baby daughter and I'm looking with astonishment as the nurse stands beside the hospital crib pointing to my child.

Now I realise that all women find all babies beautiful and that's fine. I however am more pragmatic owing to the fact the midwives must have been trying for ages with the forceps before the caesarean because my baby's head looks elongated and skinny instead of round and chubby.

I give a grin and a thumbs up as the nurse mouths 'beautiful' through the glass but I'm not convinced. My apologies to my daughter if she's reading this but many years later I would watch an alien bursting out of John Hurt's chest and it would give me terrible August 18th, 1970, flashbacks.

The very next day I'm sitting with my daughter in my arms and feeling very much the proud dad. Her head is back to normal and she really is beautiful. I'm sitting at Sheila's bedside. We've been trying to finalize the name and tucking into the bag of grapes I'd remembered to bring with me. We've gone through all the usual names... Morticia, Grizelda... Cruella but they just don't stick and we end up agreeing on Sharon. It would be a close-run thing between Sharon and Sarah but it would be Sheila's mam who had the final word and decided she was a Sharon indeed.

So that's life doing its own thing I muse to myself as I sit that evening in the Bebside Inn with my dad and Sheila's dad wetting the baby's head. I've given up on the cigar that Sheila's dad Harry gave me because it was like smoking a rolled-up jockstrap. But in my head I'm thinking that a mere ten years ago I was running around the Morpeth Road schoolyard playing cowboys and Indians with my pals and our only slight worry being next year's eleven plus and a crack at going to Blyth Grammar School. Now I'm married and a dad and I haven't a clue what to do next.

Perhaps if I just have a few more of these pints the answer will magically pop into my head. But there again... maybe not.

CHAPTER 18

Light My Fire

——————————◆——————————

It's 1973 and life is chugging along quite passably. It's not fantastic by any stretch of the imagination but happily it's not doom and gloom either. We've settled into a comfortable routine in our Salisbury Street flat Sheila and I and it's been quite a while since I've had one of my downer episodes. I've been working the past eighteen months at a firm called Atkinson Throwsters on the Cowpen Trading Estate. The money is good and I enjoy the shift pattern too. Twelve-hour shifts with three on and four off for the first week then four on and three off for the second. I really enjoyed the job and the workmates – Peter Ferry, Robbie Wright, Billy Blyth, Herbie Burnett, Jim Leighton and Bill Guyan. That was the first and only time I enthusiastically embraced a collaborative environment. Usually I preferred working alone but that period saw me fitting in as one of a team.

Home life too was fine. Sheila had been picked to represent Blyth in the 'It's a Knockout' TV programme and she would go training whenever she was able. If I wasn't working or pushing a pushchair around on my days off I'd follow Sunderland whenever I could and my dad and I had seen one of the most brilliant football nights of all time when we watched the lads beat Man City 3-1 in a fifth round FA cup replay at Roker Park. In the next round we knocked out Luton and the scene was set for the semi-final against Arsenal at Hillsborough... I couldn't wait.

I'd been picking up as much overtime as I could manage on the Superset machines to pay for semi-final day. The team working the machines next to ours had a two-man shortage and overtime was there for the taking for several months. So all in all life was good at that point and that fact in itself should have been cause for concern because in my experience life had a habit of not allowing itself to be good for a prolonged period of time.

It's the week before the semi-final. I've already arranged for Robbie Wright to cover my shift on semi-final day and I'll do a shift for him sometime in return. Excitement is building and I come in for my six o'clock start on dayshift with only ten days to go before the match. The foreman pulls me to one side and tells me that a new starter will be coming in at eight o'clock. He will eventually fill one of the spots on the team that are two operators light but they won't have the time to train him so it's left to the day shift lads on our team. So that means myself for today then Pete Ferry will take over when I begin my three-day sabbatical before picking up my four night-shifts. I don't mind because I had to go through the same training regime when I started. I just hope that the bloke is keen and capable of picking things up quickly.

I was working away... head down as I tied in a whole side of yarn. It was something that had to be done quickly and expertly otherwise you ended up with dropped ends and then had to re-thread each individual station and that was a pain in the butt. I could see out of the corner of my eye the foreman waiting patiently with the new lad at the top end of the Superset. They waited until I'd finished the tying in and when they saw me stand up from the little doffing trolley they came down the aisle towards me. I just gawped and you could have slapped me round the face with a kipper.

"Jim... this is the new lad I want you to train up."

"Sidney Brown," I said. "Just my luck ehhh?"

"So you two know each other?"

"Aye... we do. Just leave him here Dick I'll show him the ropes."

"Good man Jim... go and have a smoke and a coffee."

It was Sidney Hawky Brown and he hadn't said a word. He looked extremely embarrassed to be standing there waiting for me to show him how to go on. "Come on Sid," I pointed to the area door, "let's do what the man said."

I led the way to the bait room and Sid followed.

The conversation at that point could have gone two ways. I could have belittled Sid after his outburst at my twenty-first last August when he was telling all those who would listen how he was going to set the world alight when he finished his final year at Oxford University and how he felt sorry for those of us stuck in a sad little dump like Blyth. On the other hand I could just sit back and wait and let Sid come to terms with his current situation and then give me some sort of explanation. I chose the second option. I didn't want hassle.

"Coffee Sid?"

"Aye please... white with sugar."

I brought two coffees over from the new vending machine. I sat down and took out a packet of State Express and lit one up. I didn't offer Sid a smoke but that was the extent of my revenge. Sid took out a packet of Rizla's and a chewed half-ounce packet of Golden Virginia and began rolling an extremely thin tab. He made a pig's ear of the roll up. He looked sheepish and self-conscious as he lit it up. He immediately began coughing.

"On the rollies now Sid?"

"I don't smoke... not really. I just need something to stop me feeling crap."

"Tabs aren't the answer Sid."

"Naah I know," he said and stubbed it out. That was the one and only time I ever saw Sid smoke.

I made no further comment. If he had something to say then he'd have to pick his own time. We sat in silence while I finished my tab then...

"Come on drink up and I'll show you how to tie a weaver's knot. It's the most important thing you're likely to need here so learn it well." With that we headed back to the machines.

Sid picked up the idea pretty quickly as I expected and I followed him around and watched as he tied in dropped ends. "No Sid... remember it's left over right and under then right over left and tie."

"Aye sorry Jim I forgot for a second." Then he completed the tie-ins without further mishap. That was the extent of my teaching for the present time and it would be up to Pete on the following day to show him how to feed the yarn through the nip-rollers and spinner peg on the Superset. That was the hard bit and had to be done with a dexterity which was difficult to pick up. However that wasn't my problem and apart from the instructions I gave him Sid and I talked very little during the shift.

Four o'clock came around and that was the end of Sid's shift. Mine would continue until six o'clock when my night shift release turned up... a lad called Harvey. I was about to take my leave of Sid in the bait room before returning to the machines for my final two-hour stint.

"D'yer fancy going for a pint tonight Jim?" Sid asked but didn't make eye contact. That had come out of the blue and was unexpected because we'd hardly exchanged a personal word all day.

"Can't Sid. Babysitting duties tonight. Sheila's going to a practice thing for the 'It's a Knockout' team." As soon as I mentioned Sheila it changed the whole tone of the conversation. Sheila and Sid had taken an instant dislike to each other at my 21st birthday bash.

"Aahh okay nae problem." Said Sid and that should have ended things but for some reason I felt bad for my old mate even though he'd been so obnoxious last time we'd met.

"I'll be in the Joiners tomorrow night for a game of darts if you fancy popping in Sid."

Sid smiled. "Aye right... see ya then." Then he was off. His shift was over for today but he left in a happier mood. We'd soon see what tomorrow night would bring.

Sid appeared in the Joiners at about eight o'clock the following evening. None of the darts crowd were in apart from Eric and Derek and they were hogging the board so I was sitting nursing a pint on my own. Sid saw me sitting alone as he came in and he headed straight for the bar. Two minutes later he was putting two pints of Tartan and two packets of scratchings down on the table. He sat down and smiled.

"Where's your pals?"

I grinned, "Obviously short of cash. Payday tomorrow isn't it?"

We sat and drank for a few minutes without speaking. I took out a cigarette and sparked up. Making conversation with Sid wasn't easy anymore. In our pre-teen days you couldn't shut us up but the last five or six years had seen us drift an ocean apart. I didn't know how to kick off the conversation but it still came as a shock when Sid did the honours.

"I was kicked out of Uni Jim. I know you've been wanting to ask why I'm working at Atkinson's."

Wow... that statement hadn't been expected. I thought Sid may have been using this job to generate a chunk of cash before taking up a contract with a prestigious law firm or something. Maybe a way of lording it over us sad Blyth folk. But kicked out of university? I thought if you were caught cheating or plagiarising you had to resit the exam or at the very worst you were sent down for a year... not completely ditched.

"Wow Sid that must have been some serious cheating you did to be kicked out. Were you copying stuff straight from the Britannica."

Sid took a big mouthful of beer. He dropped his eyes before replying, "It wasn't for cheating it was for theft."

"Ehhh?"

"I stole some cash."

Now that scenario I just couldn't imagine. Sidney Brown stealing... naah there had to be more to it than that."

"Come on Sid I don't believe that one. You might have been a bit of an arse at times but you've never nicked anything in your life."

"Three hundred quid." He answered but still didn't make eye contact.

"What... did ye rob a bank or something?"

"Pinched a wallet from my friend's dad."

"But why?"

Sid took a few seconds to formulate his answer, "Because my friends were all rich or their families were well off and I didn't have two pennies to scratch my backside with."

"So how did the nicking thing happen?"

"There was a party at my friend's house in Berkshire. His twenty-first. His dad's an MP you know... Conservative and they're loaded. Their house is like a manor house with about twelve bedrooms and portraits all over the shop. I just did it. I saw a wallet and pocketed it."

I didn't know what to say. Sid nicking stuff didn't sit easy in my head. Why was he knocking about with the rich kids anyway?

"I don't get this Sid. Is your mam struggling for cash or something?"

"No she's doing well."

"So was she not helping out with money while you were at Uni?"

"Yeh of course she was... but what we call money and what the rich kids call money are two completely different things."

"So why didn't you just ditch the rich kids?"

"I couldn't. I'd borrowed too much and got in too deep with the smart set. They thought my mam was into chemicals."

"Well she is."

"Aye but they thought she owned a chemical plant... you know like ICI but a little bit smaller. They didn't know that she sold washing up liquid and bleach from a shop and door to door."

"So you lied to them?"

"Not really. They just assumed when I said chemicals that a manufacturer was what I meant. I didn't lie I just didn't correct them."

"Same thing though isn't it Sid. So you started borrowing money?"

"I had to because when we went for a night out they didn't drink pints they used to drink expensive cocktails in the posh clubs and sometimes even champagne. I couldn't keep up and so I said my allowance was only paid in every six months. Then they lent me money to be paid back when the allowance arrived. I managed to pay back the first time. I won't tell you how... suffice to say I haven't spoken to mam for almost a year. Then when I knew I couldn't repay the loan money last time... well I saw a wallet and took it."

We sat in silence for a while. I was honestly in shock.

"Have you been to court then?"

"It never made it to court. I don't know why but the charges were dropped. I think mam and Michael her husband got involved. With him being a policeman it wouldn't have been good for his career if the theft thing came out so I'm assuming that they paid the money back and did some sort of deal but I don't know that for sure cos I'm too scared to contact them."

"So what are you going to do now Sid?"

"I don't know... I really don't."

"Well forget about looking in my direction if you're wanting a loan. I'm just getting by and I've a family now."

"I'm not after money Jim. I just want to keep my head down and get my life back on track. I've been thinking of looking Milly up again."

"Well good luck with that one Sid.

"I'm living in Shankhouse just now. So I'm going to straighten my life out and see where that takes me. And by the way sorry about your birthday bash. I had a lot on my mind."

"And my fist in your face."

"Aye that an' all." I don't know why but Sid smiled at the memory.

"It wasn't funny Sid."

"Nah I know but it's a slice of life we'll both remember. It taught me a lesson too. I'll be keeping my trap shut in future."

He was certainly right about that... my knuckles still grimaced at the memory of Sid's hard nose end. We left each other that night with neither of us knowing that the next time we met there'd be tears involved. One of those Tug moments was about to change our lives completely.

It's 17th April 1973 and I'm at Hillsborough for the FA Cup semi-final. Tonight is meant to be a night-shift for me at Atkinsons but that is being covered by Robbie Wright. I'll be covering his morning shift tomorrow and then we'll be all square. Sid finished the last of his training days yesterday and will be picking up his first regular shift tomorrow. We'll be working quite closely together and I'm sort of looking forward to it. I think that maybe life has taught Sid a huge lesson and if he's taken the message on board then maybe we can be proper pals again. I certainly hope so.

The bookies in Sheffield were raking in money that Saturday or so they thought. They were laying odds of 4/1 and more against Sunderland beating Arsenal and there were long queues of Sunderland fans outside their betting shops. We'd hear rumours afterwards about some of the bookies closing their doors for a few weeks and some of them even going bust... but you know how rumours are.

What can I remember about the match? Very little as it happens apart from seeing Charlie George's Arsenal goal squirm over the line after a save from Jim Montgomery. I was right behind the goal and I remember a sinking feeling in my gut. It was now 2-1 to Sunderland and still the best part of ten minutes to play. I couldn't look and I remember a few of the blokes around me pushing their way out through the crowd because it had all become too much for them. They'd go and wait underneath the stand and just listen because this had become too dramatic and they couldn't risk their eyes seeing another Arsenal goal... that would be too much to bear.

Then the ninety minutes were up... the whistle blew and Sunderland had reached the Cup Final. We wouldn't leave the ground. We jumped and hugged and laughed in a state of complete disbelief and the noise was just humungous until finally Bob Stokoe came back out of the tunnel and acknowledged the massed ranks of Sunderland fans. I couldn't even cheer at that point because I was so hoarse but it was a moment I'll never forget. It was a day to remember.

Unfortunately huge happiness is usually the precursor to devastating sadness and so it would prove that evening.

"Tell me ma' me ma'.

We won't be home for tea.

We're going to Wemberlee.

Tell me ma' me ma'."

The bus back home was rocking and those of us who could still sing did so. Those of us who were too hoarse just mouthed the words and got stuck into another can of beer. We'd just achieved the impossible and who knew but maybe... just maybe we would be able to progress that one further step come the 5th of May. Sunderland winning the cup? Nah... it's not possible... is it?

We were nearing home and our state of euphoria had now quieted into a happy acceptance of our achievement. The singing had stopped a while ago and now fitful snores were the only noises breaking the silence. I'm sitting beside a young bloke called Gus who I see quite often at the Morpeth branch of the Sunderland Supporters meetings. He gives me a dig in the side.

"Hell of a blaze going on ower there. Must be some sort of explosion at Bates Pit or something."

In the distance there's a huge fire. It's miles away but so bright that it's unmissable. We can't make out exactly where the blaze is centred but Gus is probably correct about it being around Bates Pit. Folk on the bus gawp for a few minutes but there's nothing we can do about it apart from murmur about hoping no-one has been hurt. Then we settle back down for the last few miles and forget about it. I'm looking forward to some proper shuteye.

It's the next morning and although I've only managed a few hours' sleep I'm due to go into work and cover Robbie Wright's shift as part of our swap. But there's a knock on the bedroom door. I've slept over at my mam's house because Sheila has been staying over while I've been down in Sheffield. It's my nephew Billy at the door.

"You don't need to go into work Jim cos there's been a fire at the factory."

The words take a while to filter through and they come as a shock but at the same time I'm pleased because I can now have a few more hours in bed before going over to see the extent of the damage... cos I'm still knacked and hung-over. I'll need to go and find out how long it's going to take to get the factory cleaned out, fixed up and back to normal... and maybe we'll have a buckshee couple of weeks holiday to look forward to... but for now a couple of hours sleep won't hurt.

It's late morning pushing for early afternoon as I walk down Edendale Avenue and then take the little cut through between the old folks bungalows onto Cowpen Road. Look both ways then across the road and over the waste land towards the factory. But I stand for what seems an age, just staring at the factory... because it isn't there. The factory isn't there anymore... just a smouldering pile of bricks and timber and destroyed machinery. My stomach churns and my heart sinks. I know what's coming.

There's a little crowd gathered around where the office part of the building used to stand. I go over and join them. Herbie Burnett and Robbie Wright are standing with a group of lads who work the machinery at the far side of the plant. I don't know them very well but all faces look the same that day, sullen shocked and glum. Sid's face appears from behind Herbie and it's tear stained. Several of the lads indeed have tears in their eyes. This was the best paying job in Blyth at the time unless you were underground on the coal face. Sunderland and the semi-final have been quickly forgotten.

The strange thing is that I'm welling up myself and a couple of sneaky tears escape before I manage to pull myself together. I should be inside the building that doesn't exist anymore working my shift and boasting to everyone in the bait cabin about the Sunderland match but instead I'm absolutely gutted. This is the first job that I've ever felt comfortable in. The first job in which I've ever felt relaxed whilst working as part of a team. I don't just feel sad about the end of the factory and no doubt the end of my employment but I have an awful sense of foreboding. This is not a good day.

We all stand around for the next half-hour or so being glum and saying glum things. Then Herbie suggests we all retire to the Traveller's Rest for a few pints and a chinwag. That sounds like a good idea because tomorrow will be signing back on the dole day and none of us are fancying that. A few of the lads have cars but most of us decide to walk to the pub and give the cobwebs a chance to clear. I walk down there with Sid, Billy Blyth and Robbie Wright. We don't say much. We're all mulling over private thoughts.

The atmosphere is somewhat morose in the pub as we pull two tables together for the gaggle of disappointed operators. There is a sense of disbelief that our lives have just changed big style and life isn't going to be the same for any of us. Two pints later however and we've cheered up. Robbie Wright has already decided he's going to give Alcan a crack. Apparently there are jobs going. It wouldn't suit me though because I don't have a motor and it's quite a journey. Ted the shop-steward reckons on going to work for Arrow chemical company as a sales rep. The power station gets a few mentions and there's even talk from some of the lads about going back to the pits. There are lots of different ideas being bandied about and I quite fancy the idea of trying Brentford Nylons. They are always on the lookout for new operators especially operators with previous experience. So things begin to look and sound more promising but deep down I know that this change of circumstance isn't going to be doing me any favours whatsoever.

"What about you Sid?" I ask.

He shrugs, "I don't know. It's a bit of a kick in the teeth. I've only been there five minutes so I won't even get a reference. It's fortunate that I only have myself to worry about. What about you Jim?"

"God knows. I'll give it some thought when I've let it sink in. It's not ideal is it? A wife and two bairns."

"Two bairns ehhh...you've got two? I didn't know."

"Aye... there's two right enough... Sharon and Deborah. It takes a man to produce lassies... or that's what the blokes who haven't managed to pop lads out keep telling me."

"Bloody hell Jim, two bairns... you need to tie a knot in it."

"Nee chance of that Sid... it's not long enough."

Chuckles from both of us and it's the first time we've laughed together for a few years. It feels good but surreal.

"Anyway Sid it's a complete nightmare this whole getting older and taking on responsibility stuff. Sometimes I miss the years of Grammar school and no responsibility... just wondering how to raise threepence for an Embassy and a light at Charlie's shop."

Sid replied, "I hated Grammar school Jim. I don't trust anybody who looks back on those years from 14 to 18 and says they were enjoyable. To my mind I think if you liked being a teenager, there's something wrong with you."

"Aye I suppose," I said, but that comment had come as a surprise.

"So do you fancy having a crack at Brentford's?" Sid lays down the question.

That question rears its head much too early for a sensible reply. At that point I was still trying to come to terms with our burned down factory and an unwelcome but indisputable life change. An answer was required nonetheless.

"Aye maybe but we'll have to sign on first and then see about the wages that are owing. You never know we might get a bit of a bonus. They've always been alright on the cash front. Anyway if all else fails I could still get the ladders out again. It's always been a decent earner."

No decisions were made that day. We stayed in the pub until closing and then took leave of each other. The beer hadn't made me feel chipper it had left me with an empty feeling in the pit of my stomach. Life had just turned naughty again and my head was going in the same direction.

That same evening back at our Salisbury Street flat we sat and talked Sheila and I. My kids Sharon and Deborah were bedded down and for some reason we had a bottle of sherry. We'd filched one of my mam's ham and egg flans and as we ate and drank we talked with an honesty which neither of us had wished to confront during those preceding few years.

Sheila wasn't happy in fact she was distinctly unhappy. She'd missed out on all her daft late-teenage years and the 'It's a Knockout' gig had made her realise she was still a young woman and not just a mother and wife. I wasn't happy because I'd missed out on a big chunk of my daft years too. I think both of us knew we were drifting and that it could only take us further apart.

So what were we going to do about it and how would it affect our lives? Did we like each other? Yes and it would have been great if we'd continued our lives as good pals. But we hadn't and we were now married and not handling it well. Staying together was an option of course but the very fact that we were sitting down and planning an exit strategy made that a non-starter. We'd jollied along together whilst the job at Atkinsons had kept us in funds and apart for long periods. The twelve-hour shift pattern and the overtime had boosted the funds but we very rarely went out together now and for quite some time we'd been ignoring the obvious unhappiness. We very probably would have continued in the same vein had the fire not brought our lifestyle to a full stop. It may well have sorted itself out in the longer term but there again maybe not. It was sad but at the same time it was honesty surfacing and we realised that we were not in fact going to be able to go the distance.

Two years later we were divorced and going our separate ways. It wasn't ideal... it wasn't even good but it was what it was and we had to get on with it. Sheila would go on and live her life in Bebside with our two daughters while I would career around for the next ten years with my constant cycle of huge highs and depressing lows dictating my life pattern until I found Charlie again... but first I was destined to plodge through some bad years.

CHAPTER 19

These Boots Are Made For Walkin'

After the factory fire and an initial period of signing on jobs came and went with monotonous frequency. Initially back on the windows... then Brentford Nylons, Shield Packaging in Washington, Dunlop Tyres, Bridon Fibres on the Team Valley before another crack at the potatoes. Oh how well had Blyth Grammar School prepared me for working life. Tug hadn't been too far from the truth of the matter.

Then one day came the job which would eventually lead me to Hull then on to Charlie and salvation. I'm sitting one evening reading the job adverts in the Evening Chronicle and one particular entry catches my eye. 'Trainee managers required for nationwide shoe manufacturer and retailer. Must be educated to graduate level. Age range 21-25. Applications initially in writing please to Stylo-Barratt Box X'.

Now that was something that would suit me I thought to myself. I can finally use my education to good effect. The only problem being of course that I'm now almost 28 years old and I'm not at graduate level whatever that is supposed to mean; and I'm also something of a drifter. No problem to a man of my calibre of course because I'm in the initial stages of one of my energized episodes and ready to knock doors out of windows. Some extreme truth bending is going to be required as I sit down and construct my application letter.

Two weeks later I'm invited for interview in Newcastle.

My first ten minutes of interview with a completely bald Mr Bright who couldn't have been much more than thirty years old had been pretty standard fare. The usual questions had surfaced... school, university, family ties and commitments, inside leg measurement, future ambitions. I'd answered them all with my usual veracity and was waiting for the big stuff... then...

"And at almost twenty-five you are at the top end of our age requirement James. What makes you think you would be a seamless fit for our management programme?"

At least they'd fallen for the 'I'm only twenty-four ruse'. I'd been worried that they'd question my age. I had indeed given some thought to turning up in short trousers and school uniform.

"Well sir" ... and I called him sir because I knew it would massage his ego. I realised early on that a bald thirty-something would respond enthusiastically to some ego stroking. "Basically I think my life experience would be a huge asset to the company. It's not as if I'm chasing my first job with blinkered eyes."

"After graduating from Oxford and working with UNICEF in various countries but predominantly the English-speaking African countries I came to realise that however we are dressed and however much property we own or money we possess we are all just human beings trying to navigate our way through life as best we can." I paused for effect, "So with that in mind every customer who walked through my branch doorway would be treat with the utmost respect no matter what my eyes told me about the state of their clothes or their assumed financial situation."

Mr Bright gave me a thoughtful stare "Which countries James?"

"Sorry?"

"Which countries with UNESCO?"

I knew he'd ask and I'd done the preparation.

"Lesotho... although it's still commonly referred to as Basutoland. There were several brief spells in Kenya and Uganda but Lesotho was my stamping ground for most of my time out there. I was based just outside Maseru the capital and we carried out our educational work throughout the country."

"Dear me that was a formidable assignment. Not something I would have fancied. How did you stand the heat?"

"Surprisingly sir it isn't a typical African state. There is nowhere in the entire country below 1000 metres and the weather is surprisingly close to the British climate. Most of the vegetation because of the elevation is Alpine and farmland is at a premium. But with the country being landlocked and completely surrounded by South Africa it is somewhat isolated and their educational establishments are rudimentary and dysfunctional."

Mr Bright sucked on the rubber end of his pencil deep in thought then looked up and smiled. "I think we've heard enough James to give us food for thought. Many thanks for coming in today and we'll be in contact in the next week or so." With that he stood up from his desk and offered his hand. I shook it and made sure to press on the middle knuckle as I did so. He gave another smile and my interview was over. Ten days later I received my job offer. The money wasn't going to be fantastic but I was in the midst of one of my cloud-nine phases and in my mind this was the initial step on the ladder of progression towards eventual world domination.

But first things first I was desperately in need of a new work suit. My existing suit had seen much mileage at various weddings and birthday bashes and was now looking somewhat fatigued. I'd had to borrow a suit for my interview and that was not a nice feeling. However I was not in the healthiest fund situation so I'd have to see if I could blag one on tick.

I can't remember how I managed to blag my suit from Burtons with just a small deposit but it was a smart navy three piece and I looked the part. I strutted about in my new togs at the Joiner's Arms in Blyth for several nights before beginning my new career with Stylo at their branch in the Galleries in Washington.

Four months working at the Galleries under a manager called Gordon Liddell set me on the road to my own branch. I'd learned how to cash up the till. Then all the stock and the codes and to be honest it was mainly boring but that was about to change.

My first posting to manage my own shop was to a branch in Middlesborough which stood right next door to Rea's café and I'd pop in there quite regularly to see if I could spot Chris Rea who was making a name for himself in the top guitarist music business. This posting was reckoned to be a poisoned chalice because it was a sales branch. Unsold stock of unpopular shoes would be shipped into the Middlesborough shop then marked down and sold off at cost price. It was not a good start but that first winter would give me an unforeseen leg up the ladder.

Dozens of boxes of Derry boots had been delivered to my branch for several weeks and the stock room was now at bursting point. I'd quickly become bored with shoe selling. Those boots looked precisely what they were... cheap and ugly and aimed at the bottom end of the market and now my branch had to sell the damn things.

The shop was not in a popular spot for shoppers being but a stone's throw from Ayresome Park and trade was sparse to say the least. My wages just about covered my pub needs and I was living in a freezing cold flat with one of those electricity slot meter things which gobbled money like a Lancashire lass gobbling pies. A single bar electric fire was my only source of heat so I would keep warm in the local pub until closing and then return to the flat to brave an icy bed with icy sheets. My life of entrepreneurship was certainly not turning out the way I'd envisaged.

Then one day the big fella up in the sky decided to toss me a bone and give my career a kick-start.

There was a little flurry of snow as I left my flat on the day we received a final lorry delivery of Derry boots. There were tons of the flaming things together with other assorted unwanted stock. I was beginning to be really annoyed at being the manager of the Stylo shop which was nothing more than a glorified rubbish dump. Then fate took a hand

and by the time we'd accepted the load... checked it and then put the offending boxes away it had begun to snow... and snow hard.

The last week before Christmas and I'm raking in cash like a casino croupier. It had snowed most of that week and in a moment of inspiration I'd marked out a three-word advertisement with a fat indelible ink pen on the clean side of a cardboard box bottom 'Derry Boots Here' it read and I placed it right in the front of the display window and it was so effective. It certainly wasn't company policy but I wasn't bothered. It did the job.

I only had two full-time sales staff working in the shop and also a part-timer on a Saturday but I'd instructed that they should be attempting to sell a pair of slippers with every pair of Derry boots. If not a pair of slippers then a can of leather spray for the boots even though they didn't remotely resemble leather. They must have thought I was a real plonker but results improved. My instructions didn't always work but sales went through the roof for that brief period of time and we became the most improved branch in the whole of the Stylo empire. We all worked so hard for that week and the shop was constantly crammed with customers who'd heard on the grapevine about our stocks of the now popular Derry boots. Requisition orders would come in from head office and some of the bigger branches which had depleted their stocks of the boots. Those orders were ignored and binned.

Every last pair of Derry boots were sold before the Christmas break and a last-minute visit from the area manager gave me a brilliant pre-Christmas boost. The daily sales figures were so impressive it had been decided that I was ready to handle a big branch. After the Christmas and New Year period was over I would be taking over a branch in Hull of all places.

I was looking forward to handling a decent branch but I hadn't counted on Hull. I'd been thinking Manchester or Leeds or maybe even London. But Hull it was and it would require my best shot if I was to impress the powers that be and progress further up the food chain.

How can I describe my first impressions of Hull. I can't really because I've tried to keep bad language to a minimum and the town comes as something of a shock when you're unsure what to expect. I was without wheels at that time so I had to use the train to transport me and my suitcase of belongings to my new adventure. That in itself was a bit of a pain because I couldn't get a direct service on the day before I took over the branch and had to wait ages for a Hull connection at Selby station.

Coming in on the train was similar I suppose to coming into Baghdad after the overthrow of Saddam. It looked dank, drab and third worldly with dilapidated rows of ramshackle houses and graffiti all over the shop. The town was smelly too with the overwhelming aroma of fish. Imagine the North Shields fish quay but a hundred times bigger with the smell inescapable.

I'd booked into a cheap hotel for a week and that first evening was spent unpacking my case and then having a stroll around to find my bearings. I didn't stray too far from the hotel because it wasn't in the most salubrious of areas but after a brief wander I found myself in a pub called the

Mainbrace and whiled away a few pleasant hours with my hands wrapped around a pint glass.

The Stylo outlet in Whitefriargate was a complete opposite to the tatty shop I'd just vacated in Middlesborough. This one was clean and slick with deep display windows and the kind of up to the minute stock that had been no more than a pipe dream at my first branch. As I walked in to take over my new assignment and saw the eager faces of my new staff I thought to myself 'I'm going to enjoy this gig' this should be a doddle.

Doddle it was and as boring as hell. Within a week I realised that I wouldn't be with Stylo much longer. Standing around for eight hours a day in a suit might seem a desirable assignment to most folk but I quickly tired of the monotonous nature of the job. Open up the shop... sell some shoes... clean the shop... balance the till... cash up... shut the shop... spend wages... repeat ad nauseum. Within a fortnight I was scanning the Hull Mail for job advertisements and before a month was out I had three interviews lined up.

Needler's sweet factory was the first to reply closely followed by Smith and Nephew and finally BP Chemicals. BP at Saltend was one of the most sought-after jobs in the area and they turned out to be the first of the trio to schedule an interview... and the first to offer me a job. And so began my Hull years or the wilderness years as I've come to regard them.

I'd spend the next three years with BP and quite happily as it turned out until my huge downer and then my eventual meeting up again with Charlie. My life took on some substance then thanks to that old fella. But that next period of life after Charlie is for a future telling.

CHAPTER 20

Postscript – It's All Over Now

‑ ❊ What happened to Charlie Chuck and who was he really?

Well Charlie lived until he reached the grand old age of ninety-three which is nowt but a toddler in biblical terms. Was he in fact a real person? I've been asked that question by numerous readers of 'A Funny Thing Happened in Blyth'. Yes he was a real person. Was he British? No but he did serve in army intelligence after escaping Europe in the early years of WW2. Did he really have a big pools win? Yes, very big and this author ended up being a grateful beneficiary of his largesse. He was a unique and kindly old fella.

When I turned up for Charlie's leaving evening I discovered that he'd beetled off the previous day. He hadn't wanted any fuss and honestly I hadn't booked a stripper or anything. I was disappointed but the very next day I received a substantial cheque in the post at my Glencoe flat and a goodbye letter in a very spidery handwriting. For the life of me I can't find that letter and I've kept it for years. I've probably put it somewhere safe... but I can't find my 'safe' place. Aahh well... old age and dry-rot catches up with all of us. The letter however to the best of my remembering went something like this.

"Dear James, my apologies for the little deception. Unfortunately I've never been accomplished when it comes to goodbyes. I always handle them badly for some reason and for that I'm truly sorry. Perhaps I need some of your new pills... ha-ha. You will find enclosed a small investment in your future success which I'm sure will happen very soon. Use it wisely and head back to your homeland as soon as possible. If you bump into Sidney or Marjorie let them know I am still alive and kicking and think of them often and say hi to your dad too. James you and I will meet up again, I'm certain of that but as we said a few days ago 'don't leave it too long'. If you move on and vacate your current address please make sure you have your mail re-directed. I will send you my new address and details as soon as possible.

So my old friend and protégé... keep well, keep smiling and be successful. Most of all James find something that makes you happy. A job or a place or a good woman. If you have the money to go with those things then fine and dandy but always remember that happy trumps money every time."

Here's looking at you kid... Karol.

Charlie's cheque was substantial and opened up new horizons. Some of them would prove successful and some not so much but it did furnish me with the foundation on which to build a future.

Would I see Charlie again? Yes, but it wouldn't be in Sweden and it would be another four years before we met up again. I'd also get to meet Charlie's nephew and his family and spend a few glorious days catching up and laughing at the past. My old mentor was very frail by then and we both knew that we were experiencing our final goodbye moments. He did however still like a drink and could bend his elbow with the best of them. He was also smoking like a chimney much to the annoyance of his nephew's wife but Charlie was past being lectured. When he finally went to meet his maker I'm sure it would have been with a cigarette in one hand and a large malt whisky in the other.

I didn't attend Charlie's funeral. It was close family only and Charlie had insisted on a non-religious affair. He was however a pathfinder for humanist funerals with a simple plywood coffin without the flashy handles and floral tributes. He was laid to rest as he had lived... a simple man after a simple life leaving behind a simple message. 'Happy trumps money every time'.

*Hull after Charlie.

Did I leave Hull as requested by Charlie asap? Well not quite. My asap took four years and two of those years were a little ropey to say the least and two were extremely successful. The ropey years included several business ventures which didn't turn out quite as intended with a few dodgy interludes involving freemasons which are maybe consigned to the 'official secrets' box.

However there came a day when funds were fairly depleted. I hadn't up to that point used the Charlie money as wisely as he envisaged. So I'm sitting in a pub called the Priory Inn one day chatting to Wendy the landlady. I'm bored so I begin reading the classified ads in an Exchange and Mart someone has left on the bar. I'm hoping for inspiration. That inspiration wasn't going to come from my beer however

because it was a Hull brewery pub and their beer was awful...
imagine drinking sprout juice through a tramp's sock. Then
I spotted the advert that was to make me a pile of money and
set me on a collision course with the tax man.

"Ex page 3 lingerie surplus sale stock. Most items in
original packaging. Must be able to collect. No delivery
service. Contact... and then a Nottingham phone number.
At this point I was driving around in a Bedford van doing
various bits and pieces of work so I had the required transport.
I used the payphone in the Priory and within a few minutes
I had arranged to be in Nottingham that very evening with
cash in hand.

I'd stumbled upon stock that had been advertised in the
Sun newspaper and modelled by their page 3 girls. There
was a load of the unsold stock but I was expecting to have to
pay a decent chunk of cash to secure the whole lot. When
I arrived at the Nottingham address and asked how much
the guy wanted I was shocked. He wasn't even asking half of
what I was expecting to pay. That immediately set the alarm
bells ringing but even so I told him it was far too much... so
very sorry but I wasn't interested. I turned to walk away but
I'd noticed desperation in the bloke's voice and he quickly
called me back. An hour later I was leaving Nottingham with
a van load of lingerie for which I'd not even paid a third of
the expected amount. It did cross my mind that it could've
been nicked because the guy seemed desperate to have it
out of his house and away in my van but who was I to cast
aspersion. I'd been sensible enough to write out a receipt
with his address on and have it signed so that covered my
backside.

I remember singing along to the radio all the way back to Hull. That was the day that the 'Night Shadow' lingerie company was born and two riotous years were to follow and much money was made... and spent but that tale is for another volume too.

*Tax man.

It would be the tax man who finally kick-started my return to Blyth. I thought that I could outrun them. Maybe they were just interested in my tax affairs in Hull and would give up if I moved far enough away. Not so folks. I'll tell you all about it at a later date too but can you believe it?... those people were wanting a share of my hard-earned money. Now I'm no mathematician but the tax demand that landed on my doormat was absolutely huge... it didn't make sense. I think they'd mistaken me for someone rich and famous so I decided to change the location of my doormat.

I thought that would be the end of it but not so. Batesy was going to have to be fairly elusive. It was going to take a huge amount of cheek and two alarming court appearances before I could rid myself of these government highwaymen but first they had to find me... and that's a tale and a half.

*Back to Blyth

I finally made it back to Blyth in late 1988. I lodged for a short period of time with a bloke called Cecil. Even that short period was too long because I discovered we didn't have the same interest in the fairer sex and I wouldn't realise that until I found his stash of magazines... featuring scantily clad men doing scantily clad men things. A few riotous months would ensue with the Folly at Shankhouse featuring heavily as I attempted to give that pesky tax man a body swerve.

Eventually he would track me down via my Insurance number and my stall on Blyth Market. That happened in the same week that I met my wife Lorraine in the Rex Hotel. That too is a tale for a future telling.

*On to Walker (Newcastle)

Four weeks after meeting Lorraine we were living together. A few months after that we were on holiday in a place called Sidari in Corfu and two months later Lorraine was baling me out as the tax man finally had his pound of flesh. However I managed to shrink his pound of flesh to a few ounces and I escaped that confrontation intact. After that episode we were never apart as a couple and we're now approaching our thirty-fifth year. Business ventures came and went during that time but with my sensible tablet head on and we even set up a football club... Walkergate Rangers based at the Fossway pitches and stocked with a bunch of players from Shieldfield club... and we'd even end up with three different kids' age-group teams and also the first embryo girls' team... and it was all hard work. There would be a few confrontations with various locals during that period... a drink-driving conviction, undeserved I may add, and finally a new-found career with BT.

*BT

BT took seven years of my life but it proved extremely lucrative and suddenly all those years of struggle became a doddle. Someone up there was looking after me and I've often wondered if Charlie and Tug had met up and put their heads together. I still made regular runs to Blyth... usually on a Sunday to meet up at the Duke with my dad on a Sunday morning. BT though provided not only a good income but also memories that make me laugh even as I think about them. One riotous week on a training course in Stoke stands out.

During that period I tried to track down Titch but he no longer lived in Dene View Drive and I also tried to look Sid up but he was no longer traceable in Morpeth. I found his mother Marjorie but she'd washed her hands of Sid and didn't know where he was living. We'll share all of those memories too.

*The Highlands

Finally we made the best move ever. A heart attack changed our life focus so we sold our house in Walker (Newcastle) and bought a cottage way up in the north of Scotland. The cottage was a few miles outside of a place called Tain and for seven years would be our hideaway and where we'd have a final week with Hawky. Then we were glad to move to our current location in Sutherland because of neighbours who had bought the house next door to our cottage. I hope they had a good life... aye... and pigs might fly.

Those eighteen years with all the ups and downs and frequent trips back to Blyth for funerals and other family events will be released in early 2024 as volume 3 and will finish off the 'North-East Diaries trilogy. It is my profound hope that you have had a super reading experience in following the trials and tribulations of Sidney (Hawky) Brown and his family, Batesy and Titch, Charlie Chuck and Jesus, Tug... Mordy and Taps, Raisbeck and Scone, Bill Taggart, Wilf Rees and all the other Blyth folk who have made an appearance... not forgetting the Blyth Grammar School folk in all their glory. They aren't just my memories... they're yours too.

*Vol 1 – 'North-East Diaries' A Funny Thing Happened in Blyth is always available on Amazon – ISBN 978-1802278613

*Vol 3 – 'North-East Diaries' The Times They are A Changin' is currently being written and continues the story to the present day.

*Bramble and Bruce a Westie's Song will be available before Christmas on Amazon and other sites. Paperback and eBook availability. A preamble and the first chapter are shown on the following pages. If you're a dog person give it a read. It's a dog's life from a Westie's point of view.

Bramble & Bruce - A Westie's Song (Introduction)

Hi folks, I realise that some of you who are taking the time to read this preamble to my memoir... in all probability, and quite understandably aren't ready for a book about dogs... and authored by a dog. If that is the case then read no further and return to your elves and pixies, quidditch and weird railway stations for they are interesting too. If however you can unleash your mind and accept an offering from our oft abused but forgiving animal kingdom, then read on... for this is it, my book, or my Westie attempt at it.

I appreciate that canine-phobia is rampant in the UK and English-speaking world because of the widely held belief that any life form with four legs and a hairy body with the inability to communicate verbally must be thick and stupid. Not so human people... it's a complete misunderstanding...

we're actually more advanced than you think. My human family taught me those things... and they taught me about the disparity between talk and action. The huge political promises and the disappointing results. I point you to the Trumps, Johnsons and Putin's of this world to allow you to draw your own comparisons. Who indeed is on a higher plane... and who should be classified as lesser life?.

To be fair that same attitude is not so rampant in other parts of the world because we're a non-entity... a commodity and an afterthought. In many places basically, we're food, and actually a delicacy in parts of China, and areas of Russia and the far east... how disgusting is that?... because it would never cross my mind to eat human flesh. Myself and my kind are far more advanced than that. We believe all life is sacred... 'don't you?'

I actually have a story to tell you. It's my story, and it may not be fantastic or violent enough for you. I have to admit that once I chased a rabbit and killed it... and my human mam was terribly upset so I never did it again. After that I still used to bark at the little buggers and warn them off... and I even chased them, but I never took the life of a rabbit, ever again. This tale may not be on Netflix or Amazon for murders are at a premium, no superheroes or alien invaders, and not a single fairy, elf or wand, but at least it will be true and not fantasy. This is my story, my life story... it's as I remember it, and as true as I can make it while my last hours play out in the arms of my human mam and dad. This is my song... my Westie song... I hope you like it.

CHAPTER 21

Hello/Goodbye

───────────────■───────────────

So here I am a West Highland white terrier I've been reliably informed and I'm sitting in a big brick pen with all my brothers and sisters. The humans call this time February 2008 and they tell me I'm six weeks old now. But the truth is I'm really sad because I haven't seen my mam for over a week and I miss her scent terribly. The last seven days have been awful and I've had a little cry and a whine to myself on a night-time... but it hasn't helped and she hasn't re-appeared. I know she's okay because I can hear her and smell her, so she must be close but the humans aren't letting us puppies be with her. Apparently it's all part of the separation process... but what do I know?

All I know for sure is that I'm not having mam's milk anymore and I'm having to eat some disgusting sloppy porridge mess out of a dish on the floor. I don't like it at all and can't be bothered to fight with my siblings to get at the yucky offering when feeding-time comes around. This lack of fight has prompted the boss human who is in charge of us Westies to give me my official name... he says I'm 'Runt of the Litter'... and that makes me very proud because none of my brothers and sisters have official names yet. So, I'm not 'Sniff 7' anymore. I must be a very special Westie indeed.

Yesterday 'Sniff 6' my brother left us to go off with his new family and educate some humans. Unlike me he hadn't been given a name before he left and we just recognized each other as 'Sniff 6' and 'Sniff 7'. We said our goodbyes just before he was taken away. Our boss human lifted him out of the pen and handed him over to a woman person... his new mother to be.

"Hello Hamish... you look like a Hamish," the woman took hold of my brother gently, then she snuggled him into her bust and gave him a human kiss on top of his head. She seemed nice and in desperate need of some doggy affection. "Welcome to our family you little darling." The lady had tears in her eyes. Sniff 6 looked over to me and head winked... he looked happy... he'd certainly fallen on his paws. I head winked back and sent him his final thought message, 'see you around brother, take care' then in a blink of an eye he was gone and I would never see him again.

As for the thought message thing... we Westies, and all other dogs too... or so I believe, communicate with scent first of all, then we use dog telepathy... talking to each other in dog-speak, head-to-head, no barks or words needed. Thoughts and emotions go from one head to another and we understand it... it's simple and we're born with it, and much better than the human alternative. I was soon to find out that humans don't have this ability and they can only communicate with a complicated mish-mash of hand gestures, face pulling, and barky noises that they call chatting... how complicated is that? And in all of my fourteen years I've never once seen two humans sniffing each other.

My other siblings were 'Sniff 1' my brother and believe me he was the real tough pup of the litter, then 'Sniff 2, 3 and 4' were my sisters, and finally 'Sniff 5' who was also my brother but like me he wasn't tough and I worried about him... a lot. He was scrawny like me and there was something wrong. He'd told me a few times that he felt poorly. I'd sniffed his bum and that told me he wasn't kidding... he was indeed poorly but I couldn't make the big human man understand. The very night before I left to join up with my own adopted humans I cuddled into 'Sniff 5' and that made him happy.

Night quickly became morning and I certainly wasn't expecting to be next to leave on that particular day. I was the 'special one' after all, and one of my sisters told me that she'd heard humans always save the best till last, so I reckoned that being 'runt of the litter' would definitely mean that I was the last to be picked. Maybe boss human would even think about letting me stay here with mam.

Good news though. Very early in the morning, while it was still dark outside and even before the stinky porridge was served up, a big human with a funny hat came to see my brother 'Sniff 5'. He had a big box with him and a long tube around his neck. At the top of the tube were two funny white things and he put these into his ears before using the bottom bit of the tube to press on my brother's chest. I was surprised because my brother didn't wriggle or anything... I'm sure I would have. Then the big human shone a little light into 'Sniff 5s' eyes, pulled his lip up to look into his mouth and then turned him around, lifted his tail and poked a little silver tube up his bum. After a few seconds he took it out, shook it, then gave it a hard stare before smiling. I wasn't pleased when he smiled because I certainly didn't think it was funny.

I was sitting as far away as I could and kept my bum hard to the floor in case he came for me with his silver tube, but he didn't. Instead he filled a different tube with some milky liquid and squirted it into my brother's mouth. Then he took out another tube with a long skinny spike on the end... then pushed the spike into my brother's haunch and squeezed the top end of the tube. I had to look away because I thought it would hurt him but my brother didn't flinch at all. I thought he was being very brave.

Then the funny hat human went to talk to our regular boss human and they barked at each other before doing that smile thing and shaking paws. Our boss human picked up my brother and took him away into the place where he lived in his own kennel with his human bitch and puppies. I didn't know what had just happened but I had a feeling that it could be something good.

Indeed it was something good. Before the day was halfway through, who should be placed gently back in our pen but 'Sniff 5'. He was bouncing about like a mad thing and jumping all over us. They'd made him better. One of my sisters told him off about the jumping, she even gave him a nip, but to no avail, he was just happy to be back with his family again. I bounced over to see him and I asked him if he was alright. For an answer he jumped on my back and we rolled around on the floor for a while having a play fight. He was so happy that day and I was happy too so I let '5' win.

Dogs can't smile like humans but he gave me a head grin and told me he was feeling on top of the world. All the humans in their big kennel had been making a fuss of him and he'd slept on a blanket in front of a big fire. One of the human puppies had stayed with him and gave him some big cuddles until the white medicine worked. Then when he was feeling better they gave him a big dish of special food... not porridge, and another squirt of milky medicine. I was pleased for my brother, and it gave me a much different opinion of the big human who looked after us... he was alright.

Food came next and I was starving so I had a few mouthfuls of the awful gruel but that was as much as I could manage before feeling queasy. I'd even given some thought to pretending to be poorly so that I could have some of that nice food in the human kennel but honestly I couldn't be bothered. I knew that soon I'd be exchanged for lots of sheets of human money paper before going off with some sad two-legged person who was desperately in need of some Westie therapy. That was my job and our mission in life... to make sad humans happy... or so mam had told all of us puppies.

Then it happened... the meeting that was to change my life. I hadn't made any plans for this... how could I. I was a puppy for heaven's sake and I'm looking back at those days with all the information that I have now as a fourteen-year-old. Back then I was just a normal mad-head pup who didn't even know how to scratch at the door when I needed a poo... I just did what I had to do whenever I felt the need... and then let the daft human folk clean up after me... that's what was meant to happen, wasn't it?

On that eventful morning the first time I saw my human mam and dad I wasn't impressed. Mam looked friendly enough, but dad... or the man who was to be my new dad looked like a total grouch. He didn't even smile when he was talking to our boss human, and he had an older male Westie with him, on a lead, and to be honest he looked even grumpier than the man and it seemed like he wanted to be anywhere but here. I immediately understood the situation and tucked myself away in the furthest corner, as far away from the speculative parents as I could manage. I tried to look anywhere but at those two humans. These people were nothing like my real mam... they didn't have enough hair or legs and they smelt funny, but I was intelligent enough to understand that like it or not two-legged folk like this were to be a big part of my future.

I'd heard all kinds of stories from Gizmo... our boss human's dog when he sneaked in to frighten us pups with his terrifying stories... but I knew he was just showing off, or at least I thought I did. Because if all his stories were correct about dogs that he knew... who were being kicked and bashed with sticks, starved and left out in the cold and rain, then how come Gizmo had such a shiny coat and a nice bed? Not only that but he also went out for walks and holidays and got to eat really nice food with chunks of meat in it... so his stories just didn't ring true as far as I was concerned.

So on that particular day I reckoned it must be time for one of my sisters or perhaps my brother 'Sniff 5' to find their new human family to supply with joy. I watched out of the corner of my eye with interest as the lady moved around the outside of our enclosure. Like typical madcaps two of my sisters ran up to the wall where the lady was standing and tried to clamber up but it was too high. The lady reached over smiling and stroked them but for some reason she had her eyes fixed on me... or possibly '5' who was crouched quite close by. She did one of those people gesture things to our regular boss human and pointed to me... and it was definitely me. I pretended to be uninterested. This lady obviously wasn't aware that I was special... the 'runt of the litter' and because of that I should be the last to go... who did she think she was? Then I thought to myself... maybe she's special too and that's why she's recognised me. She must be important.

She was important... and so was my new dad, extremely important. I didn't realise it at that moment but they were about to give me a life that many of my dog friends and family could only dream of. A life full, not of things or fancy houses and cars, or designer collars with shiny diamonds... or any of the other possessions that humans hold dear... but a life full of love and cuddles, vet appointments and walks in the countryside, fun and games in the back garden and on the beach... and total devotion. I was meeting a human family for the first time, but if any of my canine peers have had a better life then I congratulate them because I couldn't imagine how life with my human family could have ever been improved. Mam and dad I love you both.

Okay enough of the soppy talk. Anyhow on that fateful day I realised what was coming when I was picked up by our regular human, quite gently as it happened, and I swiftly sent my telepathy goodbyes to my brother and sisters. I heard all of them reply and one of my sisters was actually crying... I don't know why, it must have been a girl dog thing. Then I was put into the arms of my new mam. I was a little nervous and frightened at first but she smelt nice and she cuddled me in and stroked my head. I relaxed too quickly and had a wee. I thought that maybe she'd put me down after my little mistake and pick one of my sisters instead. But she didn't.

"Oh you little rascal Bruce," my new mam chuckled and smiled as she held me in one hand and dabbed at the wet patch on her blouse with a handkerchief. "That was a lovely greeting."

"My name's not Bruce," I head shouted, trying to get my thoughts out of my head and into hers, but I couldn't, her head was closed off and I couldn't find a way in, "My name's Runt... Runt of the Litter... honestly, just ask the boss human... he knows."

Regular boss human didn't say a word. He could have corrected her but instead he was busy counting through a pile of money paper that new dad had put in his hand. Counting finished he put a bigger piece of paper in new dad's hand and said, "That's the pedigree and registration... and I'd advise you to take out insurance as soon as possible."

New dad paused and thought hard for a few seconds, "Why is that?... he's not the runt of the litter is he?"

"Nah, of course not the runt went yesterday for half price. It's always best to have insurance for your dog... is all I meant."

New dad seemed satisfied with that but I was desperately head shouting, "Eeeh, you big liar, tell him the truth... you know I'm 'Runt of the Litter'... let new dad know that I'm special... 'new dad', 'new dad', it's me... Runt, don't believe that liar. You're lucky new dad cos you've got the special one."

Regular human turned away with his bundle of paper and didn't say a word. He didn't tell them the truth and I was disappointed because he didn't even come over and say goodbye to me... or even let me say goodbye to mam... perhaps he wasn't alright after all.

Thirty minutes later and I'm in the back seat of a car. New dad was driving and new mam was sitting between two Westies. Myself to her left in a little basket with a nice soft pillow and a cuddly blanket that had little dog pictures all over it. Before we'd left she had fastened a little blue tartan collar around my neck and I thought it made me look special. To her right was the older westie she called Bramble and he was lying at new mam's side with his head on her lap, a red tartan collar around his neck, and he was staring hard at me. I don't think he was too impressed. I tried not to look back at him.

The journey was long and awful. I was sick twice, poo'd once and wee'd lots of times. It was my first time in one of the car machine things and I was really frightened and started to cry but mam cuddled me in and made some nice noises. They were sounds without words which I'd later find out were called lullabies. New dad was being grumpy in the front because he must have been tired. We were driving from near Aberdeen to my new home beside a place called Tain. It was an awfully long way and he'd already had to drive that same journey in reverse.

We stopped several times for a rest and a wander around outside... 'to stretch the legs' I heard new dad say and at each stop mam gave me a dish with some milk and some nice tasting porridge. It was nothing like the awful porridge at my puppy home. The other Westie, Bramble, ate some meaty strip things and only drank water but he kept well away from me and seemed annoyed at having to share his mam and dad. Only once during one of our stops did he bother to give me a sniff and for a brief second he allowed me to sniff back... but he wasn't happy. Maybe he was insecure... but that was no excuse, at least he could have said 'hello' to me or something.

One funny thing though was that whenever we stopped for a rest, new dad would get out of the car then lean back against the closed door and put a white stick into his mouth. Using his paws he would make some fire come out of a little machine he'd taken out of his pocket. Then he would put the fire up to the white stick and give it a big suck. After a few seconds he would blow stinky grey clouds out of his mouth and go "Aahh... that's better." I think he was just showing off but I was really impressed.

It seemed a long, long time before we arrived at my new home. It was called Northwilds cottage and it was in the middle of nowhere. I'd fallen asleep a few times in the car and I remember I had some awful dreams. What if Gizmo had been telling the truth and this new mam and dad were just pretending to be nice before they started with the stick hitting stuff. But every time I woke up mam would give me a cuddle and do the lullaby noises... and she smelt nice apart from where I'd had a wee on her blouse... so I felt safe.

When the car finally stopped, and our journey was over I was really scared because it was pitch black... I couldn't see anything except the stars up in the sky, and it was so cold and icy. New dad got out of the car first but this time he didn't do the stick in the mouth routine. He moved away into the dark and made some rattly noises with some shiny things he took out of his pocket. A few moments later a light came on, a really big one, and it shone brightly on the outside of the place they called home.

New mam waited with me in the car until new dad returned. He opened the rear door at Bramble's side first and lifted him out of the car before putting him down on the ground. Bramble didn't wait around in the cold, he ran straight into the cottage through the open door. Then new dad came around to my side of the car, opened the door and picked up the little basket with me inside it. "Time to see your new home little fella," and with that he carried me into my forever place. Maybe new dad wasn't so grouchy after all. Mam closed the car doors and followed along behind.

That first night in the cottage put all my fears to rest. I was really hungry and thirsty and mam made some really lovely food. I gobbled it down quickly and then sneaked across to Bramble's bowl to see if there was any more. Bramble warned me off... then did a head speak with me for the first time. "You can't have the same as me Bruce. You're not old enough for grown-up food so don't even think about nicking any or else you'll have me to deal with." That sounded ominous and Bramble looked a lot tougher than even 'sniff 1' so I backed away and lay down. But I wasn't happy with the name thing.

I was only little but I wasn't having that, "You should call me by my proper name... it's Runt of the Litter, not Bruce"

I head-shouted, "Why can't you all call me by my proper name?" I protested.

"Don't be stupid," growled Bramble. "Runt of the Litter is a silly thing that humans say to each other and it means you were the weakest of the puppies... the one they wanted to get rid of, and that man was just being awful to you... and don't ever let mam and dad know... they're nice parents and they would be upset if they ever found out," then he gave me a long hard stare, "and never let mam and dad know that you can understand human talk... okay? I'll tell you why tomorrow when we're outside." Bramble left it at that and went to lie down in front of the fire that new dad was setting.

Mam came through into the front room with a big damp cloth and some disinfectant and began rubbing at the carpet where I'd done a wee. Then she went to the back door that led into the garden and she put down a white pad just inside the door. Something was going on, something special but I wasn't frightened anymore, I knew these humans were alright. New mam came and picked me up and carried me to the pad and set me down on it. It smelled funny and it made me want to wee again... so I did. Mam clapped her hands and gave my head a rub, "What a clever boy you are... that was so clever," then she shouted through into the big room, "Jim, Jim, he's just had a wee on the puppy pad, come and tell him how clever he is."

I heard the grumping noise from the front room as the Jim dad roused himself to come through and view my success. He was talking under his breath but my hearing was so much better than theirs and I could hear what new mam couldn't. "Bloody wee on the pad, give him a round of applause, why not put an advert in the flaming paper." Then new dad appeared. "Ohhh what a clever boy you are... isn't he a clever boy mam?" Dad wasn't being sarcastic he was just trying to get into new mam's good books.

"He certainly is... he's a little star. I told you he looked like the cleverest of the litter."

I could hear a snort from Bramble in the front room. He sent me a head thought, "See if you can have a poo as well clever dick and they'll both start cheering, bloody cleverest of the litter indeed." I did as I was told and had a poo as well. Mam was ecstatic, clapping her hands and scratching my head... just because I'd done a poo, but I'd made her happy. Dad however just grunted... scowled, and walked back the way he had come... I think he was really tired out from driving the car and needed a rest. I wasn't bothered though, I was enjoying this new family experience.

Then bedtime came and that was a strange affair.

I cried and cried because I was missing my proper mam and my brothers and sisters... I didn't know if I'd ever get to see them again. I was feeling so frightened, even though new mam and dad were really nice... but my new brother 'Bramble' seemed as if he didn't like me at all... and he looked very tough. I was just a bairn and terrified about what the future had in store for me and I couldn't know how it was going to play out. I needed some affection.

I got it that night... affection I mean. New mam and dad put me in a cage thing with some blankets and a little bit of material that smelt of my proper mam. They were only being kind, I realise that now, but it made me feel even worse and I just wept like the puppy I was when the light went out.

'Mam... Ohhh mam, proper mam please come and snuggle me in... I miss you so much.'

Bramble was lying in his dog bed snuggled into a pile of blankets and he wasn't amused. "Will you shut your whining and whingeing and let them have some sleep, they've been up since early morning to go and fetch you... and you're crying like a big baby."

"I'm frightened Bramble... frightened, I'm not big and tough like you... I want my mam."

Bramble seemed pleased with my tough comment and took a little while to have himself a good think, "Okay Bruce... tell you what, give it some really big whines and squeaks and I'll do the rest. I can remember what it was like on my first night... don't worry about it... just do some more crying stuff and I'll tell them to give you a cuddle. I'll fill you in tomorrow on all the human stuff you need to know."

That was nice of him, he seemed to be warming to me. So I did what he'd told me. I whinged and whined and squeaked for a good ten minutes... and Bramble began to bark... I couldn't understand what his barks were meant to do, it was just dog shouting and it wasn't even proper words but I thought to myself 'I'll have to learn those bark things'... because after a few minutes they got results.

"Ohhh for Pete's sake," I heard new dad growl. "Will you do something about that noise so I can get some sleep?"

"I can't do anything... apart from bring him up onto the bed. He's frightened, it's not his fault," said new mam. She was being very diplomatic because looking back on that night... dad was exhausted.

"Put the little fella on the bed then... on your side. I don't want to be cleaning up after him. Just do it Lorraine... I'm shattered."

Shuffle-shuffle-shuffle... then next thing I knew the door of the cage was being opened and I was in new mam's arms.

"Come on Bruce... you must be missing your mam terribly," she whispered as she held me close, "I know I'm not the same... but I'll give you all the love that I can."

"Lorraine... will you shut up and get into bed for heaven's sake... I really need some sleep," grumped new dad, "I'll be walkin' around like a zombie tomorrow if you don't get him settled. I've got that fencing to put up before Billy and Michelle arrive." With that dad turned his back and snuggled down as mam cuddled me in under the fat blanket thing that they called a duvet.

Three times during that first night new mam lifted me out of bed and took me to the puppy pad. Three times I had a wee, and not once... not even once did I have a wee on their bed. I was learning quickly and knew that new dad wouldn't have been pleased if I'd had an accident on their nice duvet. I only cried a little bit because I had someone to cuddle into and pretty soon I was out like a light. My exciting day had caught up with me. I was too tired to even worry about what tomorrow might hold.

The complete Westie Tale will be available on Amazon before Christmas 2023

Printed in Great Britain
by Amazon

35426745R10169